CORSICA

By the same author

INTO CHINA
INTO JAPAN
JAPANESE CRAFTS

CORSICA
A Traveller's Guide

John Lowe

JOHN MURRAY

For Mark
with my love

© John Lowe 1988

First published 1988
by John Murray (Publishers) Ltd
50 Albemarle Street, London W1X 4BD

All rights reserved
Unauthorised duplication
contravenes applicable laws

Typeset by Inforum Ltd, Portsmouth
Printed and bound in Great Britain by
Butler & Tanner Ltd, Frome and London

British Library CIP Data

Lowe, John, *1928–*
  Corsica : a traveller's guide.
  1. Corsica—Description and travel—1981–
  —Guidebooks
  I. Title
  914.4′94504838   DC611.C812
  ISBN 0-7195-4429-7 (cased)

Contents

	Introduction	11
1	The Genoese Capital BASTIA	19
2	A Prospect of Mountains CAP CORSE	34
3	The Green Desert EAST COAST	48
4	The First Citadel BONIFACIO	67
5	Older Worlds SARTÈNE	79
6	The Imperial City AJACCIO	92
7	The Corsican Capital CORTE	104
8	A Fantasy Coast PORTO	124
9	The Faithful Citadel CALVI AND THE NORTH-WEST	136
10	The Granite Crown THE MOUNTAINS OF CORSICA	145

Some Practical Information 155
A Suggested Itinerary Around Corsica 172
Select Bibliography 185
Index 187

Illustrations

1 Bastia: pleasure boats moored in the old port   *f.p.* 48
2 Bastia: bustling food market, Place de l'Hôtel-de-Ville   48
3 Bastia: statue of Napoleon, Place St-Nicholas   49
4 Bastia: Pisan church, La Canonica, near Roman ruins   49
5 Cap Corse: quiet quayside at Centuri-Port   64
6 Cap Corse: the small port of Pino   64
7 Cap Corse: intricately woven fishing traps   65
8 Cap Corse: a fisherman making new traps   65
9 Morosaglia, birthplace of Pasquale Paoli   96
10 La Castagniccia: view through the chestnut forests   96
11 Aleria: view across Roman ruins to Genoese fortress   97
12 Aleria: stairway leading to Roman Praetoria   97
13 Bonifacio: fortified citadel high above the fishing port   112
14 Bonifacio: ornate tombs at the city of the dead   112
15 Megalithic Sartène: great dolmen tomb of Fontanaccia   113
16 Sartène: Genoese bridge at Spin' A Cavallu   113
17 Ajaccio: the port and surrounding old town   144
18 Ajaccio: statue of Napoleon in the Place Maréchal-Foch   144
19 Corte: view of the old town   145
20 Corte: the citadel crowning the old town   145
21 Porto: double bay protected by old Genoese watchtower   160
22 Porto: a diminished fishing fleet   160
23 St-Florent: statuary on a roadside tomb   161
24 Pigs scavenging for chestnuts   161

MAP OF CORSICA   24/25

All photographs by the author

Acknowledgements

I first went to Corsica with my former wife, Susan. I am grateful to her for good company and, I suspect, for doing more than her share of the arduous driving. When I came to write this book, she found the dates of our journey and other details which were helpful in planning the second tour. She also discovered an article I had written about Corsica at that time and completely forgotten.

I have talked about Corsica with various French people. I am particularly grateful to two journalist friends. Travel gives unexpected rewards. I met Sylvie Lanteaune and Bernard Poirette on Tai Shan, China's sacred mountain. Within a year we had become near-neighbours in France. Before I left for my second tour of Corsica they explained the modern political situation there which helped me to understand much that I saw and particularly the many changes in the island.

I owe a great debt to Yuki Nomura who came with me on this second tour. She kept a meticulous written record of our journey. From this she wrote the first draft of the 'suggested itinerary' at the end of this book. She also drew the map and checked many details for me. She made an important contribution to the book.

As on previous occasions I am most grateful to my editor, Duncan McAra, who has done so much, first to encourage the idea and later to improve the book in various ways.

J.L.
Cours, France
October 1987

Introduction

We had just finished recording a radio interview about a book I had written describing my wanderings through China. As we walked down the corridor the producer asked me what I was going to do next.

'I'm going to write a book about Corsica.'

'Corsica,' he exclaimed. 'That's a bit *tame* after China.'

Tame. I cannot think of a more inappropriate word in the English language to describe Corsica. The original volcanic forces which threw up this mountain of granite in the central Mediterranean sculpted a landscape which varies from the hauntingly beautiful gulfs around the coast to the savage outlines of the great mountain gorges. The island's history is no less dramatic from that moment around 1500 BC when the mysterious Torreens arrived with their long swords and daggers to subdue the unprotected megalithic people. From then on Corsica, coveted for its position and its natural harbours, was invaded by every seafaring nation in the Mediterranean, first settled by the Greeks and Romans, later raided and looted by Barbary pirates, Vandals and Ostrogoths; for seven centuries an Italian possession, first owned by Pisa but for five centuries ruled by Genoa.

At various times the Corsicans struggled to achieve independence led by the heroic Sampiero Corso in the sixteenth century and the great liberal leader, Pasquale Paoli, in the eighteenth century. These uprisings resulted not only in considerable drama but, in Paoli's case, an attempt at genuine democratic government far in advance of its time. Even today that implacable nature, which stimulated banditry and the unrelenting vendetta of the past, lives on in the present bombings and bank raids carried out by the extremists of the Corsican separatist movement, the Front de libération nationale de la Corse (FLNC), which continues the struggle for independence. Tourism has thrown a shroud of sophistication and prosperity over traditional Corsica but the granite heart of the island still shows some sign of life. In its present local politics Corsica remains alive and enigmatic.

I first went to Corsica in the spring of 1963 when I drove around most of the island. Although it was a quieter, less spoilt place then, already much of the island's traditional life had vanished though one could still see traces of it in the life of the remoter mountain villages. There was just enough left to give one some understanding of the life that had been. It was a significant moment in Corsican history for about then two new invasions started which in the next twenty years were to alter the character and the economy of the island almost as much as 500 years of Genoese rule.

The new invaders were the displaced French colonists from North Africa, a large number of them originally from Corsica. They were accompanied by many Arabs who became the labour force of their development schemes, soon to be joined by immigrant workers from Sardinia, mainland Italy and elsewhere. The most successful development was tourism. In the early 1960s tourists visiting Corsica amounted to a few thousand each year. Today Corsica has well over a million tourists each year making a vital contribution to the island's economy. More than half of the tourists, mostly French and German, visit the island in July and August.

I returned to Corsica to make a more thorough tour of the island in the autumn of 1986. Although the tourist season would be over I went back expecting to find the island disfigured by tourist developments, particularly around the coast. It is not the quiet, secretive island that it was twenty-five years ago. But then a great number of Corsicans are not as poor as they were and vines and citrus fruits are growing where nothing grew before. In most places the tourist invasion has been contained without too much damage to the environment. Along the east coast it is unobtrusive. The main coastal towns to the south and west have faced the problem with varying success. Bonifacio and Propriano have been partly spoilt. Calvi and Porto – among the most beautiful and most popular resorts on the west coast – have absorbed the tourist facilities with little damage to the beauty or character of either place.

The mountains – bastions of granite and porphyry – are less vulnerable and a regional park now protects the centre of the island, with regulations which have proved effective against most depredations except forest fires. And in the remoter countryside I saw as few visitors in October 1986 as I had in May 1963. In those seasons these less accessible places still belong to those few who make the effort to visit them.

It is more difficult to measure the changes that have taken place in the mountain towns. In the larger towns such as Corte and Sartène, popular with visitors, there is an obvious new prosperity. Modern suburbs are spread around the outskirts and in the centre there are more hotels and restaurants and a scattering of pizzerias and ice cream parlours. But behind the flourish of gaudy Cinzano umbrellas and the revolving stands of post-cards something older lingers on. In the side streets dour men sit outside mean cafés talking intensely over their clouded glasses of local pastis. Climbing the steep steps that wind up among the towering houses of most Corsican towns, the black-dressed widows still sit before their doorways on chairs too small for their ample buttocks. Their gaze is impersonal but one feels its penetration as one passes by. The scenery of these towns has changed but behind the scenes some part of an older play is still being performed.

I cannot remember exactly what first drew me to Corsica. I suspect that I had started out on that long process of collecting Mediterranean islands and, more important, a friend gave me a copy of Edward Lear's *Journal of a Landscape Painter in Corsica*. Apart from his famous nonsense verse I had a great admiration for the young Lear's paintings of animals and exotic birds, best of all his brilliant lithographs of a variety of tropical parrots. Behind the hilarity of his limericks Lear nursed a melancholy disposition which perfectly matched the sombre scene of mid-nineteenth-century Corsica. A kind of self-exile, this lonely man banished himself to the Mediterranean where his perceptive eye, through pen and brush, caught the character of a variety of countries. His writing has the immediacy of a genuine journal and for the natural scene it remains a practical and up-to-date guide and one that I used daily during my first visit to Corsica. The engravings have a gloomy splendour and capture the mammoth skeleton of the Corsican landscape but it must be admitted that it is only in his paintings that Lear is able to do justice to the bosky magnificence where the maquis and great forests enrich Corsica's granite outlines. I have to add that this admirable guide which was readily available for a few pounds in the late 1950s is now a rare book fetching several hundred pounds and, as far as I know, it still exists only in the first edition of 1870.

One thing is certain. Before I first went to Corsica I met nobody who had already visited the island and even my well-travelled friends expressed surprise that I wished to go there. Over the years I have continued to experience this indifference, which more recently has been fortified by a snobbery that the island has nothing to offer except packaged beach-holidays.

I fell in love with Corsica during my first visit. I still think that it is one of the most dramatically beautiful areas in Europe with an extraordinary history and culture adding to the rewards of its fine landscape. I number it among the most fascinating small islands of the world with qualities as beguiling as Ceylon, exotic Bali and the Japanese island of Shikoku. Ironically, only recently I read a Japanese newspaper article reporting that one area of Shikoku is planning to attract more tourists by building a replica French village. Corsica has no shortage of tourists, certainly in high summer when the attractions of beach and sea beckon.

A less amphibious kind of visitor might be encouraged to visit the island in spring and autumn when, apart from a lower sea temperature, Corsica is at its best.

I make no secret – it must already be obvious – that I am writing this book in the hope of encouraging a few more people to visit and explore Corsica and to share the variety of pleasures which the island offers. Let me say immediately that Corsica has many beautiful beaches, and everything that anyone could desire for a relaxed beach-holiday. In my account of the island I intend to give some information about such resorts, particularly the most attractive and those offering the best facilities and value. The background and historical information given in the book may also help you to choose from the many bus excursions which are offered at every summer resort.

However, this book has been devised mainly for individual travellers who wish to explore the length and breadth of the island and in the course of their journey to enjoy the scattered fragments of its history and to search out the traditions of Corsican life against the extraordinary variety of its coastal and mountain scenery. I have avoided interrupting the main text with too much practical information by separating most of this in two sections at the end of the book, one of general use, the other designed for the motorist. The book does not pretend to be an encyclopedic guide. My prime aim has been to encourage people to visit Corsica.

The first part of the book gives a general account of Corsica's long and distinctive history and the various places that have grown out of it from the prehistoric settlements to the several Genoese fortified towns. I hope that my personal impressions and enthusiasms will help to bring alive Corsican history and the traditional life of the island and to conjure up, as far as words can, a picture of the landscape.

When I came to plan the book I had to resolve a certain conflict between presenting the historical and cultural information and my wish to provide practical guidance. When I drove around Corsica in 1986, I followed an ingenious if circuitous route – taken from the *Guide Bleu* – which took in every important place, and many minor ones, in the island without ever having to double back on one's tracks. This is not easy to achieve in Corsica's mountainous terrain. At first I thought of making this itinerary the one that the book would follow. However, I soon realised that what is convenient for the motorist is not the ideal framework for presenting Corsica's history and culture. But our route, with its many advantages and a few hazards, is described in detail in the third section of the book. I would recommend anyone intending to drive in Corsica to read it before setting out.

I do not think anyone could be disappointed by the Corsican landscape. Coast or mountain, you will find it anything but tame. Nor will you ever find it monotonous. The island is small, its natural elements limited, yet the landscape unfolds with unexpected variety, given a special subtlety by the constantly changing light. The intense compression of Corsica gives its mountain ranges a grandeur far beyond their actual size. In spring, when snow still covers the peaks, my memories are alpine in scale. At the same time, their real size makes it easy for the ordinary traveller to penetrate into the heart of them. And, at the end of a gorge, where the road gives out, if you have the energy to walk a few kilometres, the remotest views in the island are yours.

The Corsicans are a unique people rooted in the granite of their island. But over the centuries their culture has been coloured by the long Genoese occupation and since the nineteenth century by French rule. Travelling about Corsica you will often be aware of this mixture and on occasions disoriented by it. You must accept that the Corsicans, like the British, are a mongrel breed but none the less individual because of that. With many historical characters and a few place-names the French have changed the older Italian-style of spelling for a French one. In the *Guide Bleu* you will find Pascal Paoli rather than the Pasquale by which he must have been called in his lifetime. I have mainly used the older spelling.

Outside the main coastal towns and a few towns in the interior such as Corte and Sartène, the other communities are so small by European standards that I have almost always called them villages. The word seems a better description of their size and their rural isolation and way of life.

I have written of the acts of terrorism carried out around the island by the FLNC, the extreme separatist movement. It is true that tourism is one of their targets but not, I must emphasise, *tourists*. Some hotels have been attacked when they were closed during the winter. I know of only one case where such an act of terrorism led to loss of life. The terrorists blew up a hotel believing it to be empty but unfortunately the family who owned it had returned and were killed. The terrorists appear to have a curious Corsican code of honour and they do not wish to alienate the sympathy of ordinary Corsicans. I have never heard of a tourist suffering at the hands of the FLNC. The reader may be reassured that well over a million holidaymakers flock to the island each summer from all over Europe, including France.

I was persuaded to write this book because at present there is no up-to-date book about Corsica written in English, either a general description or a guide. My original intention had been to write a purely descriptive travel book about Corsica but when I started to plan the book after my second journey I became convinced that the book should contain a substantial amount of practical information, particularly for the intending motorist. I hope that the final result, apart from a comprehensive list of hotels which can be obtained from the French tourist authorities, will provide people with a small but useful guide to the island with enough information about the main places of interest and adequate directions about how to reach them. I have tried to minimise the division between the descriptive text and the practical information by careful cross-referencing and full indexing. The directions in the book are all based on the Michelin map of Corsica (Sheet 90) which any good bookshop will stock or will order for you. It is impossible to drive around Corsica without it since in remoter places signposting is sporadic or non-existent.

Since my first visit to Corsica in 1963 I had always wished to return and this book has given me the opportunity to examine the changes which have taken place in the island during the last twenty-five years. I have discussed these at various places in the book and here I think I need ask and answer only one question, the answer summarising my feelings about Corsica.

When I visited Corsica in 1963 I was overwhelmed by its beauty and fascinated, if slightly awed, by the last traces of its traditional life in the sombre towns and villages of the interior. Was I disappointed by the island when I went back in 1986? The simple answer is that I had expected to be and in many ways I was pleasantly surprised how much of Corsica remained unspoilt and how, in certain ways, it had been improved by new wealth and modernisation. It is good to see the agriculture of the east coast reviving, the main towns enjoying a new prosperity and the mountainous regions formed into a national park and protected by new laws. Here and there picturesque townscapes have been scarred by new tourist facilities but overall the tourist invasion has been absorbed with little damage to Corsica's beaches or interference with the tourists' pleasure. One hopes that good planning will maintain this balance.

I must acknowledge my debt in writing this book to three others. I have made great use of the *Guide Bleu* and Michelin's compact but admirable *Corse*. Both these books are written in French and it would be a mistake to think that because they are guide books, they are written in simple French. They are, of course, written for French people in idiomatic French. If you do take one or both with you and you are not a fluent French reader, also take a substantial French dictionary.

Anyone who wishes to understand the history and culture of Corsica must read Dorothy Carrington's *Granite Island: A Portrait of Corsica*. It is not a travel book but a perceptive and beautifully written portrait of the island, its history and its people. It is a long book, dense with information but always lightened by its knowledge and perception and by a delightful enthusiasm based on an intimate knowledge of Corsica since 1948. It is a model of its kind, a classic in the literature of Corsica in any language and – highest of praise – deeply admired by all intelligent French experts on Corsica. I have been engaged in writing a different kind of book but Dorothy Carrington has been a source of information and inspiration.

I can say with certainty that if you enjoy nature, from wild flowers in the forest shade to the spectacular outline of the mountains against the sky, you will enjoy Corsica. If you are intrigued by piecing together four thousand years of history, not from great monuments, but from a variety of telling fragments, you will be fascinated by Corsica. If, above all else, you want a varied holiday which mingles pleasant food and wine with the interests of history and the pleasure of landscape, you are certain of a good time in Corsica.

1

The Genoese Capital

BASTIA

The boat left Marseilles at eight o'clock. We had been driving all day and had missed lunch. We made our way to the cafeteria on one of the upper decks. The *Cyrnos* came into service on the Bastia route in 1979. Bearing the ancient Greek name for Corsica (Kyrnos), she is a large and handsome ship, towering out of the water more like an ocean-going liner than an overnight car ferry, her immaculate white hull devouring 430 cars.

Aboard, the functional decoration everywhere reflected that no-nonsense contemporary French taste that characterises public development all over France. A hard, linear style brings plastic, anodised metal and other stark materials together, painted in sour colours to provide functional comfort and convenience. The ship's food was hardly more flamboyant, certainly not *haute cuisine*. About one notch above the French *autoroute* cafeterias and several more above the 'grub' offered on most British cross-channel ferries.

As I carried my tray to a table I could feel the engines vibrating far below. We were on our way to Corsica. But when I sat down and glanced at the neighbouring tables I realised that in a sense I had already arrived. Around me the modern population of Corsica was well represented, natives and newcomers. Even the way each group ate their steak and *pommes frites* and drank their red wine went beyond table manners to the roots of cultural differences. Someone once said that the Englishman betrays himself on the tip of his tongue. Perhaps the Frenchman reveals himself on the tip of his knife and fork.

The man opposite did not bother with a fork. As he sat down he took a large flick-knife out of his pocket and made a bucolic meal of bread, meat and wine, deftly cutting cubes of bread from a roll which he stuffed into his mouth to pad out the meat, sliced with equal skill. He could have been any Corsican peasant eating his meal among his sheep on the mountainside or watching over his pigs among the chestnut trees. His stony features confirmed such origins. A thick nose dominated his face. From it ran two deep, unrelenting lines down to a thin, silent mouth. He was accompanied by his young grandson and the boy's mother. He spoke to neither of them. The woman plied him with bread and wine and twice the man gave the child a piece of steak on the end of his knife. It was an older Corsica.

To my left were two more urban Corsicans, an elderly husband and wife of the *petite-bourgeoisie*, returning to their small, gloomy apartment in Bastia or some other town. The wife had those expansive contours common to that class of middle-aged Frenchwoman: bulging bosom, stomach and bottom somehow contained in a cheap printed cotton dress, her swollen ankles throttled by the straps of her sandals. Her husband was anonymous in a drab grey shirt and tan trousers. His face had as little individuality as his clothes. The couple could have come from anywhere between Lille and Arles except that their French had an unmistakable Corsican accent.

To my right was a more lively group, a young husband and wife with a small boy and girl. The man looked French but his wife's flowing black hair and eyes like pools of ink suggested the Arab world and the French colonisation of North Africa. When France withdrew from Algeria in 1962, many of the colonists settled in Corsica, a number of them originally from the island. This family represented the new Corsica; a new economy bringing new ways of life which create new problems as they destroy older traditions. Here, at a few cafeteria tables, was a microcosm of the Corsican social scene, needing only myself, the tourist, to complete the picture.

I was up just before dawn to catch the first glimpse of Corsica. The decks were greasy and the sea churned white around the hull, spreading out to the dark green sea, cold and flat in the last darkness of the night. To the west lay the great finger of Cap Corse and as the first light rose from the east, the broken, rocky outline of the mountains showed up against the pale sky. Clusters and strings of lights marking the coastline dimmed in the increasing light and as the boat drew near to Bastia the sun broke through with the first warmth of the Corsican autumn day.

As the boat eased into the new port Bastia was spread out below. Across the quay was the central Place St-Nicholas, a long, rectangular promenade given an exotic touch by the few tall palms that set off the lines of plane trees. The old town spread away to the south with the old port dominated by the Genoese citadel. The first glance showed how much Bastia had changed since I was last here in 1963. It was a brighter scene. The town was not only larger and modernised but the atmosphere was livelier; a more sophisticated place than the forbidding, shabby port I had known.

I have good reason to remember my first arrival in Bastia since it was the only occasion in twenty-five years of marriage when my wife had to help a drunken husband to bed. I repeat the incident here only because in certain ways it illustrates Bastia as it was in those days. With the help of our *Michelin Guide* – there was not much choice – we found a small restaurant by the old port which also had a few rooms. Our room was as functional as the chipped brown lino and an enamel bidet on a rickety stand but it was adequate. We had already missed breakfast but, anxious to make the most of our time, we set out to explore Cap Corse with a baguette and a bottle of mineral water.

It was a marvellous day but by the time we returned to Bastia and sat down for dinner I was starving. One distraught girl was serving the crowded tables. She took our order eventually and I drooled thinking about the fish soup I had ordered. All we got was a litre bottle of strong local *vin rosé*. Corsican wines had more strength than character in those days. Even wine fills the cracks better than nothing. When the fish soup arrived forty minutes later, the bottle was empty and my wife had drunk one glass. The soup was rich and delicious but at about the fifth spoonful everything happened all at once and the only clear thought in my head was a desperate need to lie down. Somehow I stumbled up the steep stairs that led straight out of the restaurant, found our room and collapsed on the bed plunging instantly into a sottish sleep. At breakfast next morning the *patron* asked with an air of mischief if 'Monsieur had enjoyed his dinner?' At least I had learned a certain respect for the local wines.

Such drab small restaurants with non-existent plumbing upstairs are now a thing of the past. Today, Bastia has brushed off the cobwebs and is grappling with the modern problems of industrial development and too much traffic. It is bustling its way into the future. At one end of the handsome Place St-Nicholas, Napoleon, in white marble, assumes the statuesque pose of a Roman emperor. A small but popular temporary motor show occupied the other end, voluble French car salesmen explaining the finer points of new Citroëns and Renaults and even a few British and Japanese models. In between, elegant and neglected, was a charming little bandstand which once must have echoed to the brassy strains of Gounod and Bizet. The pleasure of Bastia is a well-organised mixture of past and present. The strident demands of the present have not been allowed to drown out the quieter voices of the past.

Besides this marriage of old and new, Bastia gives one a strange feeling of a divided identity. Whatever the maps may say, the moment you start to wander around the narrow streets of the old town, with each step, at each sight and with each sound, you ask yourself, am I in France or Italy? The frenzied driving, the haphazard parking are French in character. The towering, tightly shuttered tenement buildings, the generous vowels of overheard snatches of conversation and a peculiar air of secrecy are Italian, recalling Bastia's Genoese origins.

Corsica was dominated by Genoa from 1284, when the Genoese took it from the Pisans at the sea battle of Meloria, until 1768, when the Genoese handed over their sovereignty to the French. Genoa was a mercantile state and from the beginning her interest in Corsica was confined largely to creating ports and encouraging the production of useful exports. The Genoese built six fortified ports – Bonifacio, Calvi, Bastia, St-Florent, Ajaccio and Algajola – around Corsica's coast to strengthen their government of the island and to defend their possession from foreign attack.

Bastia was not the first Genoese capital or the first of these fortresses. The citadels of Bonifacio and Calvi were built first and it was only in 1380 that the local governor, Leonello Lomellini, built a keep on the massive rock which rises above the old port, at that time the insignificant fishing village of Cardo. This new fortified port strengthened the Genoese hold over the north of the island, at the same time improving communications with Genoa. The *bastiglia*, the fortress which guarded the town, led to the new capital being named Bastia.

In 1811 Ajaccio, Napoleon's birthplace, was made the capital city of Corsica. This started a rivalry between the island's two main towns which continues to this day. Both towns are about the same size with populations of around 50,000. In 1975 the French government, perhaps to placate Bastia, divided the island into two administrative regions. Ajaccio is the prefectural capital of *Corse de Sud* and Bastia of *Haute Corse*. But apart from such political manoeuvres, in real terms I feel that Bastia is better organised and enjoying a greater prosperity based on the development of agriculture and tourism on the east coast. Steps have been taken to prevent rapid development from spoiling the old town. New housing and industrial developments have so far been limited to planned areas. This has protected the old town and, equally important, the landscape of mountains behind the town. Bastia is fortunate in having the wide coastal plain to the south which can absorb much of the necessary development without harming the environment. Traffic is a serious problem in a city whose streets were built with pedestrians and donkeys in mind. Bastia has built a large car park under the main square and eased the traffic to the southern industrial zone by building a tunnel which runs under the old port and the citadel. It was a major undertaking for a small town and is a symbol of the imagination and energy of Bastia's administration.

You may sit and observe the passing scene of modern Bastia under the plane trees on the west side of the Place St-Nicholas. Here the cafés and restaurants spread out their chairs and tables and the waiters dodge the traffic as they cross the road with loaded trays. The more interesting parts of the old town run south

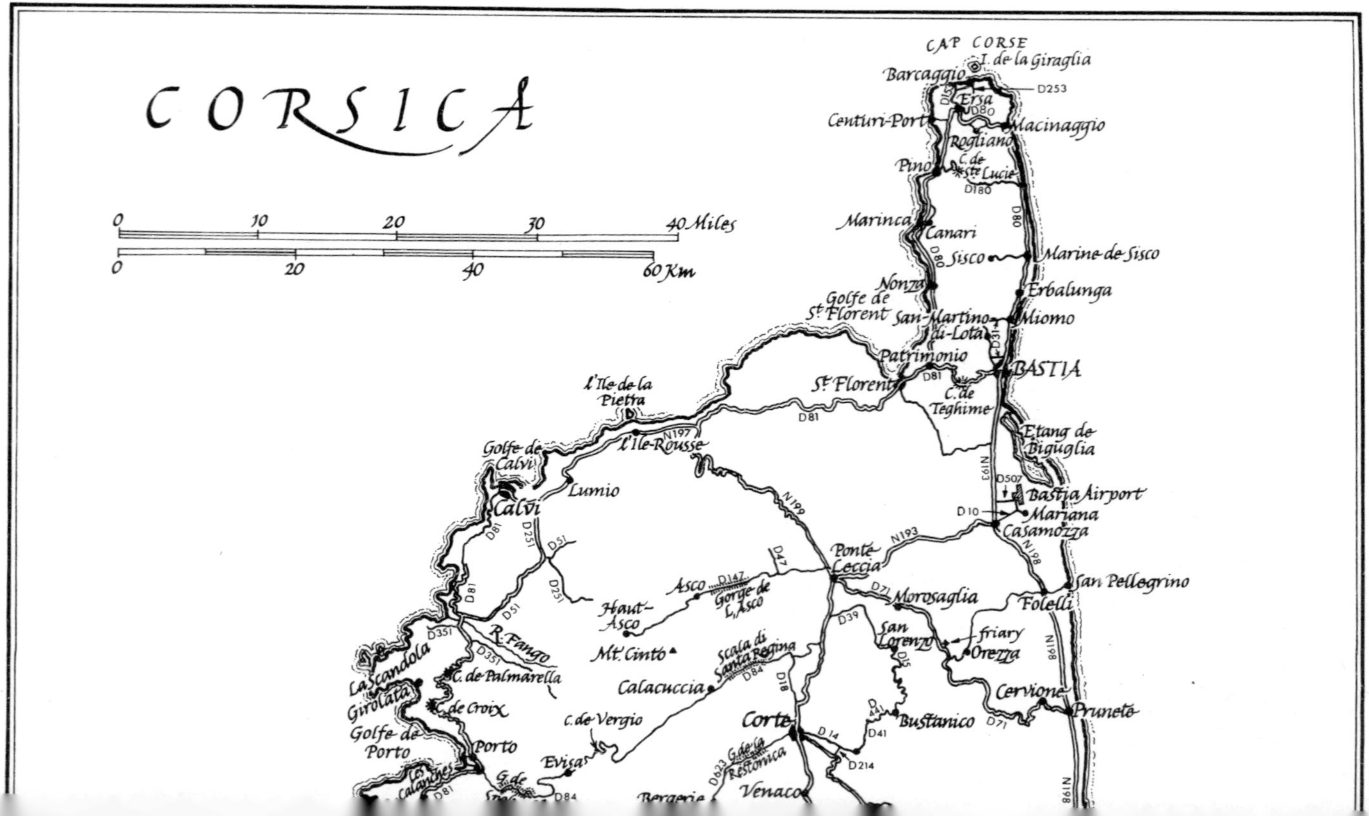

CORSICA
0 10 20 30 40 Miles
0 20 40 60 Km
CAP CORSE
I. de la Giraglia
Barcaggio
D253
Ersa
D80
Centuri-Port
Macinaggio
Rogliano
Pino
C. de Ste Lucie
D180
D80
Marinca
Canari
Sisco
Marine-de-Sisco
Nonza
Erbalunga
Golfe de St Florent
San-Martino-di-Lota
Miomo
D31
Patrimonio
BASTIA
D81
St Florent
C. de Teghime
D81
l'Ile-de-la Pietra
N197
l'Ile-Rousse
Etang de Biguglia
N193
D507
Bastia Airport
Golfe de Calvi
Lumio
Calvi
D10
Mariana
Casamozza
D251
D51
N199
N193
D81
Ponte Leccia
N198
D47
San Pellegrino
Asco
D147
Gorge de L'Asco
D251
D71
Morosaglia
Folelli
Haut-Asco
D51
D39
San Lorenzo
friary
Orezza
D351
R. Fango
Mt. Cinto
Scala di Santa Regina
D351
D84
D15
La Scandola
C. de Palmarella
Calacuccia
D18
Cervione
Girolata
de Croix
Pruneto
C. de Vergio
Corte
Bustanico
D71
Golfe de Porto
D41
Porto
D14
Evisa
D214
Les Calanches
G. de la Restonica
D623
D81
D84
Venaco
Bergerie
N198

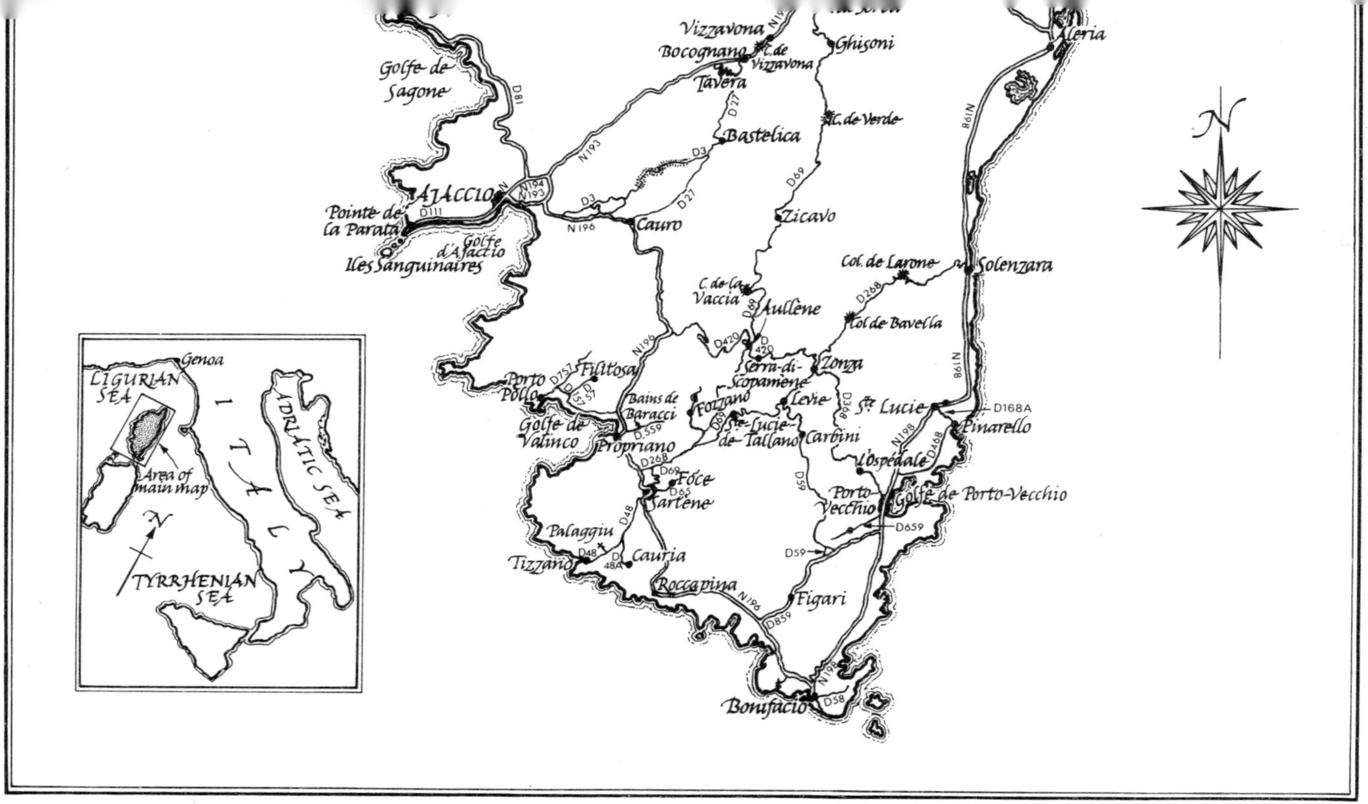

Vizzavona
Ghisoni
Aleria
Bocognano
C. de Vizzavona
Tavera
Golfe de Sagone
C. de Verde
Bastelica
AJACCIO
Pointe de la Parata
Golfe d'Ajaccio
Iles Sanguinaires
Cauro
Zicavo
Col. de Larone
Solenzara
C. de la Vaccia
Aullène
Col de Bavella
Zonza
Serra-di-Scopamène
Levie
Ste Lucie
Pinarello
Filitosa
Porto Pollo
Bains de Baracci
Fozzano
Ste Lucie-de-Tallano
Carbini
Golfe de Valinco
Propriano
L'Ospédale
Foce
Sartène
Porto-Vecchio
Golfe de Porto-Vecchio
Palaggiu
Tizzano
Cauria
Roccapina
Figari
Bonifacio
N198
N193
N194
N196
D81
D111
D3
D27
D69
D268
D420
D757
D157
D559
D65
D48
D48A
D368
D59
D468
D168A
D659
D859
D58
N
Genoa
LIGURIAN SEA
Area of main map
ITALY
ADRIATIC SEA
TYRRHENIAN SEA

from the square, first through the district called the Terra-Vecchia. This was the oldest part of the town which centuries ago started to develop around the fishing port. It takes all its character from the towering houses and tenement buildings which crowd out each other on the steep slopes around the port and lean crazily over the lanes that squeeze between them. In many places the houses have a continuing façade and there is little sense of separation. One front of peeling plaster looks much like another and the decrepitude of the wooden shutters is more or less uniform. Here and there lines of washing bring a splash of colour but it is mostly a study in greys and browns soaring up to the thin line of blue sky where rooflines almost meet.

The morning market in the Place de l'Hôtel-de-Ville brings some strident life to this quiet quarter of the town. The fruit and vegetable stalls are busy but without much interest. Further along a large caravan houses the main butcher of the market. From the canopy in front of the stall hung the head and skin of a wild boar. This advertisement was made more vivid by the snout neatly dripping blood onto a scattering of sawdust on the pavement. Boar is one of the delicacies of the island. The stall-keepers were a hard-faced lot but none more so than an old woman in a dirty brown mackintosh and wellingtons who stamped up and down in front of her stall of local products. There was home-made wine and gnarled twists of sausage and smoked ham, herbs from the maquis and honey. They all looked as unappetising as the old woman herself. Their flavours may well have been more authentic than the products offered in a bogus rustic-style shop nearby offering similar gourmet delights of Corsica, hygenically packaged and highly priced.

Although the front and twin towers of St-Jean-Baptiste look over the old port, the entrance to the church is by its east door at the lower end of the market square. Italianate in style, the church was first built in 1583 but the interior was enriched with baroque gilt and marble in the eighteenth century and later cluttered by the sombre devotions of the nineteenth century. Today, a religious gloom obscures the coloured marbles and the *trompe-l'oeil* paintings and I deplore the nasty little 'night lights' which seem to be replacing the beautiful offertory candles in churches everywhere. Elderly women dressed in black hurried in and out. As they knelt momentarily on the upright chairs they muttered into their neighbour's ear with confessional confidence. I wondered if they had come to pray or to exchange the neighbourhood gossip.

A few steps down the narrow alleys – past the hole-in-the-wall bars where the local men exchange their confidences – brings you to the old port. It is still picturesque although now more a marina for pleasure craft than a haven for fishing boats. To the east, the harbour is protected by a long mole, the Jetée du Dragon. From the end you have a superb view of the port. To the right the tall houses seem to topple against each other, rising giddily from the quay and surmounted only by the twin towers of St-Jean. Behind, the solid green mountains rise appearing almost to hold the crazy confusion of architecture together. To the left the more substantial walls of the citadel rise out of the green shade of the Jardin Romieu, heavily barred old dungeon windows half-hidden by cypress and clumps of pampas grass.

For photographers – and the old port must be the most photographed scene in Corsica – I recommend the view from the shorter northern mole which brings you nearer to the main quay and all the architectural details that give infinite interest to the view. The plain Renaissance façade of the church provides an ideal centrepiece, harmonising and in scale with the simple architecture of the narrow houses lining the quay. At street level several of the houses have been smartened up as tourist shops, restaurants and bars. Above, the houses rise in a ramshackle, patchwork pattern of life. Each storey shows the individuality of its occupants. Most of the plaster peels and blisters in muted whites and greys. Here and there a storey in canary yellow or chic pink shrieks between the precarious and rusting balconies and the cracked wooden shutters. Even in October the harbour was crowded with speedboats and small yachts. A few fishing boats were crowded in one corner. The white hulls of the pleasure boats with their blue canvas covers are matched by their own shimmering reflections and by the bar and restaurant umbrellas along the quay. The sun lights up this scene which is enchanting but hardly more real than a film set.

In the narrow streets at the north-west corner of the port you will find the main street leading back into the centre of the town. It is confusing since this street starts out as the Rue des Terrasses and suddenly becomes the Rue Napoléon. Here there are two neighbouring chapels on the east side of the street. They were built in the early seventeenth century by two religious confraternities, each determined to make their chapel the most lavishly decorated.

The Chapelle St-Roch was built in 1604 and is noted for the inlaid decoration of its wooden stalls which line the side walls. The Chapelle de l'Immaculée Conception is more sumptuous. It has an unusually long and high interior with a painted ceiling and fine wooden stalls surmounted by panels of crimson Genoese velvet while the pretty cut-glass chandeliers give a secular touch to the chapel. Gilt and marble add to the air of richness. There is a graceful pulpit of coloured marbles and a theatrical high altar ascends in steps of polychrome marble to an anticlimatic copy of a painting by Murillo. The chapel was considered the grandest place of assembly in Corsica and was used occasionally for secular state occasions during the eighteenth century. In the sacristy beyond the high altar there is now a small museum of religious art.

The curving, massive north walls of the citadel make an impressive backdrop for the old port but within and standing before the entrance to the Genoese governor's palace the fortifications look less impressive. One French guide-book observes that it all looks more like scenery for an operetta. The original fourteenth-century fortifications were enlarged and strengthened between 1480 and 1521. The new walls surrounded the area known as the Terra-Nova, in contrast to the older part of the town around the port. The new citadel encloses the governor's palace together with the large church of Ste-Marie and the surrounding maze of alleys and towering houses, squeezed together on this small platform of land.

The governor's palace now houses the Ethnographical

Museum of Corsica, a dusty but interesting miscellany of objects. They give glimpses of each stage of Corsican history, ending with a display of traditional Corsican life, rural crafts and industries. The museum appears to be run on a threadbare budget. The clumsy display cases might deter a thief for three seconds but do not keep out the dirt and dead flies which lie scattered among the objects and the faded labels. Dowdy provincial museums are always depressing, particularly when they obscure a subject of interest. Corsica deserves a good museum showing the island's turbulent history and traditional ways of life particularly as the folk material must now be in danger of vanishing for ever. The museum is worth visiting. The last two rooms illustrate Corsican peasant life and show a haunting series of old photographs which evoke the austere existence of Corsican farmers, shepherds, fishermen and their womenfolk till recent times. Their spartan life is also reflected in their crude tools, made without finesse or decoration. The plough might have come from some primitive African village while the equipment for making chestnut flour, one of the island's more prosperous industries, was basic. The peasants lived a harsh life of survival. In the photographs the granite features of the shepherds and the black-shawled village women are marked by generations of poverty and hardship. It is a narrow glimpse into the strange, introverted life of these dark people. It left me longing for an imaginative professional museum. I came out with a feeling of having visited a pauper's grave.

There are fine views of Bastia from the museum and from the ramparts of the governor's palace, over the sea and across the old port and town to the mountains. Climbing the steps to the battlements you pass a curious memorial. This is the conning-tower of the French submarine *Casabianca*. In 1942 the ship escaped from Toulon and joined the Free French forces in Algeria. Thereafter it maintained secret communication with the Corsican underground resistance until the island was liberated by French troops in October 1943. The ship was named after a young Corsican hero who at the age of twelve went down with his ship at the battle of Aboukir in 1798. His father, the captain of the vessel, had ordered his son to stay with the ship. The father was killed during the battle and the boy could not be dissuaded from obeying his father's last command. The conning-tower looks as seaworthy as a patched kitchen kettle and I wondered how such a construction had been able to submerge and withstand the pressure of the sea.

I don't know about operetta but I did think that the upper levels of the ramparts would make a charming setting for Rossini's *Italian Girl in Algiers*. Pretty gardens with roses and tumbling bougainvillaea filled the terraces folded in among the heavy masonry of the fortified walls. The embrasures were half covered by a delicate ivy and by the straggling branches of old fig trees. The only enemy in sight were the weeds taking over the patches of attempted lawn. It was difficult to believe that this 'chocolate soldier' castle had on occasion withstood violent sieges. At the start of the war of independence in 1730 4000 men from the mountains attacked Bastia. They sacked the area around the old port but were checked by the citadel. The siege was ended by the intervention of the local bishop.

The Terra-Nova – alleys leading between the high houses – huddles around the large church of Ste-Marie, built in 1495 and elevated to be the cathedral in 1570. It lost this status when the bishopric of Corsica was transferred to Ajaccio in 1801. The church was reconstructed in 1604 and the bell tower added in 1619. I cannot enthuse about provincial baroque. It is a theatrical style and like good theatre must be well done to achieve success. The large silver statue of the Assumption by a nineteenth-century Italian artist did have some dramatic quality. On 15 August each year this group is carried in procession around the citadel and the old town. The Church of Ste-Marie should have looked its best that morning. Inside the altar rails a group of women were putting the finishing touches to a bank of white flowers in front of the polychrome marble high altar. Coffin-trestles below the altar steps showed that the church was being prepared for a large funeral.

When I returned to the church for another look after lunch the funeral was in progress. The church was packed and further mourners hung around the main door or, in the case of some of the men, leant against a shaded wall and smoked in silence. The hearse was a modern vehicle, its lines hardly on the right side of dignity. Much the same could be said for its attendants. The undertaker's men wore black ties but purple blazers with a faint stripe and the monogram of their firm embroidered on their breast pockets. They leant against the side of the hearse chewing gum while within the church the choir in a rising descant helped the new soul on its way. It was bizarre; a certain Italian flamboyance darkened by Corsican shadows.

Nearby, and the least gloomy place in Bastia, is the Chapelle Ste-Croix, built originally in 1543 but its interior decorated in a charming rococo style. You could be forgiven for assuming that this had been the private chapel of some eighteenth-century dilettante governor of Bastia. However, the delicate gilt scrollwork and the chubby putti who float against the walls, holding conch-shaped torches, are the unlikely setting for the patron of the local fishermen. In an alcove hangs a wooden figure of the crucified Christ, traditionally said to have been found floating in the sea by Bastian fishermen in 1428. The seawater had turned the oak carving black. At the start of each season the local fishermen offer a part of their first catch to the black Christ. On 3 May each year a special feast is celebrated for their 'Christ of the Miracles'. The black figure is impressive, even a little sinister, and at odds with this pretty setting, more suitable for a painting by Tiepolo or music by Mozart.

The alleys of the Terra-Nova spread out from the Place Guasco in a claustrophobic maze. In places they are hardly wider than a car which does not prevent cars coming down them at considerable speed. The gloomy old houses rise up six or seven precarious storeys. An optical illusion makes them seem to topple drunkenly towards each other and suggests that only the arched buttresses between them hold them apart – buttresses and lines of washing that thrust out in every direction.

The area is forlorn yet fascinating. Apart from a grey, slinking cat and some children on a doorstep – building their dreams out of an old cardboard box – the alleys are deserted and silent. Many doors are barred and most of the shutters closed tight likes eyes that don't wish to see. There are a few occupants more curious. The tall shutters have a small lower panel which allows a discreet observation of the street below. Some of these were open a few inches and I caught a glimpse of eyes in a blurred face peering from the inner darkness.

Most of the open doorways were cavernous and decrepit stairs led upwards through uninviting tunnels of filthy walls. But on the few occasions when I did get a glimpse of a room the television set, the large refrigerator and the modern cooking stove belied the crumbling plaster of the house front. It was always said that the French never painted their houses since it only attracted the attention of the tax inspector. The quiet streets of the Terra-Nova are full of enigmas.

Not everywhere was so silent. We wandered to the edge of the area where the terraced land is linked by steps, the sea lapping greedily at the rock below. We came on a crowded school playground vibrating to the noise of the mid-afternoon break. It must have been a junior school. The girls stood apart talking. To a man the small boys were fighting. Near the lower fence one small infighter had bitten into the ear of his opponent. On a balcony, high above the action, three French teachers gazed with indifference out to sea, ignoring the do-it-yourself karate class at their feet.

There was little evidence that the rigours of junior school produced any marked improvement at more senior levels. Later that afternoon I was parked outside a bank in the Boulevard Paoli, Bastia's main shopping street. At four a human avalanche hit the neighbourhood. The local *lycée* had finished for the day and the street swarmed with teenagers. Many jostled into a small shop, next to the bank, which sold pastries and ice creams, the neighbourhood 'tuck shop'. The boys worked hard at looking tough. The girls, without effort, looked tougher than the boys. A young couple came out of the shop, their attention divided between their conversation and their cream cakes. Without a thought both of them sat down on the wing of my car, the nearest seat at hand. They had not noticed that the car was occupied. When they did glance round a minute later and saw us inside, they took not the slightest notice, finished their cakes and their conversation and departed without a nod. But the cakes looked good. We slipped in and bought a couple.

I have come to the end of my description of Bastia without any explanation why I chose this town twice as the starting point for my own tour of Corsica. Where you start will be partly a matter of personal choice but I think there are a few reasons in favour of Bastia rather than the more obvious arrival at Ajaccio. Bastia is a more Corsican town than Ajaccio and it gives visitors a useful introductory experience to the mixture of Italian, French and Corsican culture which will initiate them into an understanding of the whole island. In fact the Italian and French elements are changed into something that is entirely Corsican. Bastia is not as Corsican as the sombre port of a quarter-century ago but enough remains to give visitors their first sense of the distinct character of the island.

There is a more practical reason for beginning your tour of Corsica in Bastia. From here you can follow a route which unfolds the attractions of the island in the best order. This itinerary varies town with countryside and architecture and archaeology with natural beauty. In the countryside the places of outstanding beauty are seen in the order which ensures further variety and presents them in an orchestrated crescendo of magnificence. With a little thought and the spectacular coastline and mountains of Corsica that is not hard to achieve.

2

A Prospect of Mountains

CAP CORSE

That first morning in 1963, as we drove out of Bastia and up the east coast of Cap Corse, I doubt if we had any clear idea of what to expect. It was 9 May, a perfect day, and spring had broken everywhere. I have vague memories of the small fishing villages, cluttered working boats and men on the quays mending nets. The line of ragged mountains stood out against the clear sky from the Serra di Pigno behind Bastia to Monte Stello, the highest peak in this spine of rock dividing Cap Corse and rising to 1307 m between Erbalunga and Nonza. Compared with mountains elsewhere in the island they are not high but squeezed in the narrow boundaries of this peninsula they assume their own grandeur.

I remember our picnic best, not the baguette and the mineral water but our surroundings and the sights and scents of the Corsican spring. We stopped the car by the edge of the road. In those days there was little traffic. There was a wide verge by a small stone bridge with a thread of stream trickling away into the undergrowth. It was all here, as described by James Boswell when he passed near this spot in 1765:

> The prospect of the mountains, covered with vines and olives, was extremely agreeable; and the odour of the myrtle and other aromatick shrubs and flowers that grew all around me, was very refreshing.

Boswell was getting his first sight of Corsica and northern Cap Corse in October. Exuberant as his mood was at that moment, he might have waxed even more enthusiastic had he first seen the island in springtime. Where we sat by the bridge, within reach I counted twenty different wild flowers, some common enough, some I had never seen before. All were pretty, a few beautiful and they spread away on every side, the sun and the flowers an intoxicating celebration of spring. We were already under the spell of Corsica.

Part of the witchcraft was the famous and elusive smell of the maquis. Had not the greatest of all Corsicans, Napoleon, been haunted by the memory of that scent during his last days of exile on St Helena? Has not every writer who has visited Corsica, let alone the local poets, tried to capture the scent of Corsica's wild undergrowth? The scent has been described as sweet, pungent, bitter, heady, potent, fragrant, aromatic and resinous as incense. I have called the smell elusive because I believe that at different times and places the maquis fits all these descriptions. When I returned to Corsica in the autumn there were places where I detected a scent which I could describe only as spiced like curry.

The maquis is a dense undergrowth made up of a variety of shrubs and plants, evergreen and aromatic. They include arbutus, cistus, myrtle, rosemary, lavender, lentisk and thyme. It grows over about half the island. Apart from producing a few cooking herbs and an old refuge from the law, it is useless. It can grow to a height of about 5 m and the thorns on some plants can make it difficult to penetrate. Made up of so many plants, the composition of the maquis varies from place to place and so does the scent. In one area rosemary may dominate, in another myrtle or thyme. Part of the pleasure of the maquis is this variety and matching the changing scents to the plants around you.

I urge you to go to Corsica in the spring to see the flowering of the maquis. There is some flowering and fruiting in October but it is nothing compared to the spectacle of May. Then, with a wonderful extravagance, nature spreads acres of colour across the foothills. The four species of cystus crinkle their leaves in purple and creamy-white. The myrtle sends up tall branches of leaves among which its white flowers cluster like stars. The flowers of the asphodel float like pale blue starfish and deep purple petals break from the stalks of lavender. I do not think that anyone could forget their first sight of the maquis in full flower. Happily, that May, it was a sight with us all over the island, always beautiful, yet always slightly different.

When I set out to tour Cap Corse in 1986, it was autumn. The maquis was more subdued, cloud lay along the mountains and a few Nordic youths sunbathed where previously fishermen had squatted to mend their nets. But now at least I had more time to explore the Cap and to taste the famous local white wines made from the muscat grape. Cap Corse presents a microcosm of Corsica within its small confines, 40 km long and a mere 14 km wide. Within these close boundaries it has mountains, legends, witchcraft, history and famous men. Its emigrants have spread around the world. It makes a perfect introduction to Corsica and, visited first, avoids diminishing comparison with higher mountains, more magnificent landscapes or more peculiar traditions and history elsewhere. Cap Corse should be enjoyed first and in its own right.

On the second visit to Corsica we had our first taste of Cap Corse while still exploring Bastia. The *Michelin Rouge* recommended a quiet hotel in a beautiful position at San-Martino-di-Loto, in the mountains 11 km north of Bastia. The Hôtel Coin de la Corniche took a little finding the first time we drove up those narrow roads but the hotel and its position exceeded the Michelin description. It also proved a good base for sightseeing in Bastia. Using a different road it took only 25 minutes to the centre of the town.

The hotel was run by three elderly women whom I took to be sisters but for some reason did not like to ask outright. The youngest of the three was in charge and spent most of her time in the kitchen. The eldest and the smallest hobbled around the enormous dining room often forgetting for what she had come or gone. These lapses of memory led to muttering sessions with the middle sister in the distant corners of the dining room. They could also lead to soup instead of the ordered charcuterie. But the soup was excellent and one could not argue with those anxious, puckered eyes or the imploring 'bon appétit' that matched the look. We were only anxious that a few guests would arrive to occupy the twenty-five tables so carefully set for dinner.

The hotel was built on a terrace high above the road, looking out over the village of San Martino and the huge valley which plunges down to the sea. The houses were scattered at different levels over the ridge of land falling away to the simple church, given a charming elegance by its slender bell-tower. Several of the older houses were tall and forbidding, bringing the austere Genoese style of architecture to the mountains. This stark appearance was heightened by their crusty stone roofs which appeared to be tiled with a coarse slate. It is not slate but the schist rock from which Cap Corse and the north-east of Corsica is formed. Schist is a rock composed of layers of different minerals which split into thinnish, irregular plates. It is quarried to make heavy, rough-hewn roof tiles. They reminded me of the Horsham slab which used to be a local roofing material in that area of west Sussex.

These flaky grey roofs blend well with their surroundings. The stone architecture and the patchwork of tiles give these villages a natural texture which fits the rugged landscape. But the craft of quarrying and roofing with schist tiles was neglected, prices rose and today it costs twice as much to roof a house with schist as with the standard Mediterranean industrial orange tile. The authorities and the conservationists have realised that two or three intrusive orange roofs can spoil the character of a village. An effort is being made to reduce the cost of schist roofing and to revive its popularity. I hope that the campaign will succeed. In Cap Corse a rash of modern roofing will destroy the character of its villages. It is ironical when a traditional building material, still all around in profusion, becomes too expensive to use.

From San Martino you can drive back to the coast along a mountain road which reaches the sea at Miomo. A few kilometres north and you come to the fishing village of Erbalunga. Before the Second World War this picturesque harbour attracted a number of French painters such as Marc Bardon and Pierre Bach. It was also the place from where the ancestors of Paul Valéry's father came. The village is now a summer resort. By October the tourists had gone and the posters advertising the Restaurant le Pirate, pizzerias and discos were already peeling off the stone walls.

In the out-of-season quietness the village resumes an older

character and remains surprisingly unspoilt. Stone houses crowd around the circular port, their foundations in the sea. The *Guide Bleu* comments, 'you could catch sardines out of the windows'. A few fishing boats are tied to the quay. Others are drawn up on the grassy beach under the plane trees. To the south the port is sheltered by a rocky point of schist, skirted by foam and crowned by an old Genoese watchtower which gives a solid, martial air to the picture postcard scene. There is a slight anger in the sea which with every seventh wave hurls a sheet of spray over the long mole protecting the outer side of the harbour.

In the mountains behind the town thin banks of cloud rolled across the peak of Monte Stello but the hot sun on one's neck suggested that they were innocent of rain. One can climb Monte Stello from Erbalunga, a walk of five to six hours there and back. On a clear day there is a superb view from the summit which takes in the whole of Cap Corse. Walking towards the mountain you would pass through the canton of Brando to which Erbalunga and the neighbouring mountain hamlets belong, Brando being the main village of the area. This grouping of villages and hamlets into cantons is found all over Corsica. Along the east side of Cap Corse the cantons provide a basic organisation for agriculture and wine growing.

Cantons may also join together in certain religious activities. On the morning of each Good Friday starting in Erbalunga, a solemn procession called *La Cerca* circulates for 7 km among the neighbouring hamlets of the canton. The male penitents wear white, the women blue and each group carries a heavy wooden cross. In the evening a stranger procession is held in Erbalunga. This is *La Granitola*, the 'snail procession'. The hooded penitents move through the streets, one group in the form of a spiral following another group in the shape of a cross. The Holy Week celebrations of Corsica are unusual, related to those of Italy and Spain, but with a more sombre character which springs from the Corsican soul. The torchlit procession at Erbalunga, winding its way through those narrow streets, must be impressive and strange but there are even stranger Good Friday devotions elsewhere.

Six kilometres further up the coast, just beyond Marine de

Sisco, is the unusual pilgrimage church of Ste-Catherine, a solid, buttressed building on the mountainside high above the road. About 300 m before you come to the track leading up to the church, there is what *appears* to be the correct entrance suitably signposted by a large stone statue of Ste-Catherine. We fell into this unintentional trap and spent half an hour struggling up a steep path, snarled by thistles and brambles until this local jungle suddenly closed over the path forcing us to realise that we had reached a dead end. It was the more irritating since the church was almost in reach. Ignore the statue of Ste-Catherine and drive on until you find the steep lane that doubles back from the main road up the hill towards the church.

The origins of the church go back to an old legend. Its age is as uncertain as its historicity but it is a good moral tale. A fishing boat was caught in a terrible storm off the coast of Cap Corse. The fishermen vowed that if they were saved they would present the holy relics that they were bringing back from the eastern Mediterranean to the first church they saw. The storm abated and in the calm that followed the fishermen forgot their vow. The storm blew up again, more violent than before, and the fishermen renewed and kept their promise. And so the holy relics came to this place, a humbler church in those days.

There is no doubt that somehow or other relics of this character did reach this place. They are now kept in the neighbouring town of Sisco but for several centuries they must have attracted hordes of pilgrims to the church of Ste-Catherine as its special design makes evident. The church was built in the twelfth century and enlarged in the fifteenth century. It has a special and unusual west front to facilitate the circulation of the pilgrims and the exposition of the relics to the faithful.

Allowing for later additions and alterations it is a simple romanesque church. The west end, which looks over a large forecourt, has all the decoration and the unusual design features. The forecourt must have allowed large numbers of pilgrims to gather, sometimes for open-air devotions, at others to wait their turn to enter the crowded church. This is born out by two features on the west front. Instead of the normal large west door, there are two smaller doors which no doubt allowed the continuous flow of pilgrims into the church and out again. Above is a large arched window, now obscured by modern stained glass but in earlier times said to have been the place from which the priest displayed the reliquaries on crowded feast days. The upper half of the window is framed by a flat stone arch carved with a floral pattern enclosed by rope borders. Across the whole west façade, just above the window, is a line of carved arcades, grotesque faces and animals carved on the small corbels. As a final exotic touch, circular Italian maiolica dishes have been sunk into the plaster around the window bringing touches of blue and yellow to the brown stonework. It is an elaborate ensemble for a Corsican church and unusual by any standards of ecclesiastical architecture.

Today, any atmosphere of crowding pilgrims has vanished. The church is now joined to a forbidding stone mansion. A notice proclaims that this is a home for the retired. But the place looked deserted. Only the neat beds of marigolds and other gardening gave any sign of occupation. The place had a desolate air but the fine view across the sea saved it from being depressing. Perhaps pilgrims are now diverted to Sisco's parish church of St-Martin where the relics are kept, some in reliquaries made by local eighteenth-century silversmiths. The area was prosperous then. Now, the seventeen hamlets around Sisco have a total population of about 500 people. In the last hundred years or more, like all of Corsica, the shrinking economy and the promise of opportunity elsewhere has led many people to emigrate from Cap Corse. Men of the sea, perhaps they took more easily to life abroad. To give one example, Venezuela had a president and some 6000 citizens of Corsican origin, many of them descended from Cap Corse families.

As far as Sisco the mountains drop nearly to the coast road with only a narrow, wooded hinterland of natural terraces scattered with rock. From there on the coastal plain begins to widen, a wild countryside where the maquis grows among great outcrops of grey and orange rock. Below the road to the east the sea glitters like a blue diamond. Then the mountains fall back where a small river runs across the widening plain. At Macinaggio the road turns inland among olive groves, thick woods of oak and chestnut and the silent maquis. Here are arcadian valleys from where life has vanished. Now the old stone houses and the sheep corrals tumble into ruin, the shells of hamlets long abandoned.

Along this inland road, not far beyond the small port of Macinaggio, the dramatic panorama of Rogliano's fortified villages leaps up dark and threatening before the mountains, like a medieval army drawn up for battle. The view is revealed suddenly and overwhelms with a suggestion of menace and aggression. This was the seat of the family who ruled medieval Cap Corse. The remnants of their power form an amphitheatre of dark silhouettes against the mountains; the ruins of three castles, fortified towers, three churches and an old convent, splendid but threatening. The view appears with dramatic suddenness and it will remain in my memory as one of the most striking in Corsica.

At Ersa you leave the main road and plunge down a narrower, rougher track which winds down the wooded hillside to the small port of Barcaggio. The village was so deserted that one might have arrived at the end of the world rather than at the northern extremity of Cap Corse. The summer season had only left behind a scruffy shack by the port which in July and August served pizzas and cold drinks. We saw nobody except the occasional dog and a carload of wind-surfers looking as lost as late swallows.

The water lapped against the pitted rocks in the harbour and a few small boats bobbed on their moorings against the outer mole. The stone houses at one end of the port, their windows tightly shuttered, stood like silent witnesses to the sudden death of the place. Two kilometres due north beyond the harbour the island of Giraglia rose out of the sea, the extreme northern point of Corsica. An elongated, greenish rock, suggesting a huge whale about to dive, it has a lighthouse just at the point where the whale might blow.

We turned back, driving up another rutted, dusty track to Ersa and the main road. It was a beautiful piece of countryside. The greens of the maquis varied from liquid to polished to matt, bright with yellow autumn flowers and clustering berries. It grew dense among the dark holm oaks and the dusty silver of the olives; quiet and unthreatening but secret and secure.

Back at Ersa, having completed this 16 km diversion, we drove west again across higher and bleaker country, climbing to the Col de Serra where you have your first view of the west coast. There is a path here leading to the Moulin Mattei, a half-hour walk. A restored old windmill stands on a point about 400 m high from where there is a superb view over the north and west coasts with a series of gulfs biting into the coastline southwards. At your feet, where the mountains run into the first bay, is the small port of Centuri. It was a place of pilgrimage for me since it was here that James Boswell landed in Corsica in October 1765. The expedition was the adventure of his youth and became the subject of his first book. The whole episode was as bizarre as it was heroic and I had long wanted to visit the place where he started his enterprising visit.

Boswell had left Harwich in May 1763. Although he had only just met Johnson, his new friend came to see him off. Boswell had an allowance from his father to enable him to continue his legal studies in Utrecht. Young and restless, and frequently amorous, this modest academic excursion soon turned into an ambitious Grand Tour which kept him in Europe until February 1766. By July 1764 he had moved on to Berlin. He wrote home expressing a wish to visit Italy. En route, he argued, he would have the opportunity of visiting Voltaire and Rousseau. All his ambitions were realised and during his meeting with Rousseau, the philosopher told him that the Corsican rebel government had invited Rousseau to draft their new constitution.

It is uncertain when Boswell first had the idea of visiting Corsica, in those days as remote as Madagascar to most young men on the Grand Tour. Boswell claimed later that he had formed the idea before he met Rousseau but there can be little doubt that Rousseau's description of Paoli, the heroic liberal leader of the Corsican rebels, must have stirred Boswell's enthusiasm. Boswell had already begun to collect heroic or moral men who 'would be a treasure for the next generation'. On both counts General Pasquale Paoli was a strong candidate for this pantheon.

Boswell was in no hurry and spent the first ten months of 1765 wandering around Italy from Turin to Naples, studying antiquities in Rome, climbing Vesuvius in the company of Wilkes and making love in Sienna. But he kept Corsica in mind. In May he wrote to Rousseau asking for letters of introduction to the rebel leaders. At last, in October, he set sail in a merchant vessel from Leghorn. At that moment, under a treaty with Genoa, French troops were occupying Bastia. Boswell feared that if he landed there he might be prevented from proceeding to the rebel territory. He therefore chose a boat which would land him at Centuri from whence he could make his way discreetly to Paoli's headquarters.

Boswell was only twenty-four when he landed in Corsica. Apart from his desire to meet Paoli, the young man must have been full of a sense of adventure as he stepped ashore at Centuri. Sailors on the boat had assured him that he would be 'treated with the greatest hospitality: but if I attempted to debauch any of their women, I might expect instant death.' Boswell was wise enough to follow their advice. During his journey from Centuri to Corte he received generous hospitality in the houses of various prosperous Corsicans. He also enjoyed the simpler welcome of the Franciscans. Boswell was a lapsed Catholic but he liked the company of the Corsican friars.

In Boswell's day the small port of Centuri must have been a busier place. He might still recognise the simple outlines of the harbour framed by plain, shuttered houses capped with schist roofs. It is still a pleasant place, small houses and narrow lanes climbing up from the sea to the woods which surround the village. Even in October the village drowsed in the midday sun. In the wide bay just south of the port families paddled and sunbathed and fished off the rocks. I thought it one of the most unspoilt fishing villages I saw in Corsica but it cannot last.

Already one large hotel – concrete nesting-boxes – has been built above the village interrupting the view of the surrounding mountains. Within the town there are increasing symptoms of that architectural disease *provençal-itis*: pink stucco walls, orange tiles and shutters painted in any vivid colour that gives the occupants the sense that they are living between Menton and Marseilles. Soon the craft shops will open and it will be difficult to tell if you are in Centuri, St Ives or Sausalito.

For the present Centuri remains a relaxing place where nothing happens but one is never bored. The fishing has diminished but from time to time a small boat chugged into the harbour to unload fish and lobsters. Along one of the quays we found two men making large bell-shaped baskets of some kind of cane, each well over 1 m high. I thought that they were some kind of local lobster pot but the men explained that they were used in March and April to catch a local fish. The cane is thin branches of myrtle soaked in the sea to make it pliable. When I asked one of the men how long it took to soak it, he said with feeling, 'Not half as long as it takes to find the thin branches of myrtle.' We saw similar pots in other fishing villages but I never discovered the name of the fish caught in them. The basketmakers said they weighed about 1 kg but I think the name they used was taken from the local dialect.

The Hôtel Vieux Moulin added considerably to the pleasure and character of Centuri. A large house, well placed above the port, it may once have been the kind of seigneurial home where Boswell was entertained. It still had a distinct family atmosphere which, while pleasant, gave the service an unpredictable amateurism. The young man who took your order for a drink seemed solicitous but left you with a feeling that it might never come.

The hotel's office was also the gunroom. Racked up around the walls was an impressive array of shotguns, sporting rifles and, at the end of the row by the door, two ugly automatic rifles. This seemed excessive even for the French passion for shooting sparrows. The manager assured me that the automatic rifles were a measure of protection against the *séparatistes* who, besides robbing banks, have shown their dislike of tourism by burning down hotels. It seemed unlikely in this peaceful spot but over the centuries nowhere in Corsica has been secure from some kind of violence. The contemporary activists have Corsican qualities in common with the banditry and vendettas of the past. Boswell had hardly set foot outside Centuri before he noticed that every Corsican male was armed.

Along the west coast of Cap Corse the mountains run down more steeply to the sea forming a dramatic coastline of deep gulfs and high cliffs. Below the village of Pino, down a rough track, is another small fishing port, more rugged than Centuri. On the cliff above is the old Franciscan church and adjoining it the friary building. On the hillside by the church were three small walled cemeteries, marble kiosks for the prosperous and plain wooden crosses for the paupers. I hoped that the wild flowers might bring a greater comfort to the dead, rich and poor alike. But the rich had made their own provision. On marble slabs lay wreaths of porcelain flowers in livid colours, their glazes more exotic than any rain forest orchid. The Mediterranean has cultivated a peculiar vulgarity in death. The church was locked. They usually are in remoter places. Judging by the lines of washing, one end of the friary had been converted to a private house. Where it overlooked the sea it seemed to be a workshop. The Franciscans are long gone from Corsica, victims of the anti-clericalism which followed the French Revolution. They first came to Corsica in 1236. They were a civilising influence on Corsican life. They gave refuge and aid to the poor, the oppressed and, on occasion, sanctuary to those fleeing from the law, bandits and murderers.

Of all the great Catholic religious orders the Franciscans were the only one to exercise a major influence on Corsica. Perhaps the Benedictines and the Dominicans preferred the conveniences of mainland Italy. It is significant that when Paoli opened a university in Corte it was almost entirely staffed with Corsican Franciscans. In retrospect it seems a happy chance of history that the followers of St Francis should have taken into their care an island of such great natural beauty. It is sad to see their friaries abandoned and their great missionary churches falling into ruin. Their traces remain all over the island.

At the village of Pino, above the port, a road climbs east to the Col de Ste-Lucie and to an old medieval tower where tradition claims that Seneca, the Roman philosopher, was exiled. It is true that at the age of thirty-nine Seneca was banished from Rome to Corsica for seducing the niece of the Emperor Claudius. It is more likely, however, that he spent his time in Corsica at one of the two Roman settlements on the east coast, Aleria or Mariana. Whatever the truth, Seneca's tower, perched 564 m high, on clear days offers a view as far as the Italian coast. The road to the tower is the last to cross Cap Corse before one reaches the base of the peninsula where the main road crosses back to Bastia.

It is a spectacular drive down this coast, the road high above the sea and turning inwards where it follows the line of the deep gulfs. Just below Canari at Marinca the coast is horribly scarred for a kilometre or two by a large and now disused factory where amianthus was mined and processed for the manufacture of asbestos. This left a vast residue of grey slag which was tipped down the cliff below the factory and slid into the sea. The hillside above the factory is now a grey waste and the neighbouring beaches and shoreline have been polluted. Coming from the green world of the maquis, there is a terrible desolation about this place. It is a shock to find a decaying industrial plant on this beautiful coast. It was also an enigma. The standard French guide-books do not mention the factory and we were left wondering what this huge and grim plant could have produced. Later, I found it described in an old English guide-book at a time when the factory was still in production. The author remarked that the industrial waste had already spoilt one of his favourite beaches. The place is particularly memorable since outside Ajaccio and Bastia there are few large industrial buildings in Corsica.

A short distance further brings another shock of a different kind. The road twists and turns, then it straightens running high above the sea. In the near-distance, seeming to fill the sky, rises the great black rock of Nonza. This fierce pinnacle, towering over the town, is crowned by a Genoese watchtower, producing the dark silhouette of some monstrous fortification, the ramparts falling sheer to the sea. Rock upon rock, set on a vertical cliff, it appears as precarious as a house of cards. There is a drama in the view with an impending certainty of collapse and a thundering avalanche into the waiting waves.

In the old town is the church of Ste-Julie, patron saint of Corsica. She was crucified in Nonza by the occupying Romans for refusing to take part in pagan rituals. Her body was removed to

Italy in 734 when Nonza was threatened by Saracen invaders. She is remembered in the town by a miraculous fountain. Her church has a particularly fine coloured marble altar which was brought from Italy in the late seventeenth century. The feast of Ste-Julie's is celebrated on 22 May.

As you drive south beyond Nonza you see the huge gulf of St Florent. North of the gulf the road turns inland towards the village of Patrimonio, centre of Corsica's most famous wine-growing area. No less famous is the view of the village from where the road twists up towards the high pass of the Col de Teghime. The sturdy little church is elevated and slightly isolated from the village. The biscuit-coloured stone is marked with the original scaffolding holes and the church gains height and a rustic elegance from its belltower. It stands above the houses of Patrimonio scattered over the slopes and framed by the chequered green patterns of the surrounding vineyards. They are strung out in neat lines across the valley, their symmetry a symbol of the careful husbandry that has brought fame to the wines of Patrimonio. It is the perfect view of a perfect Corsican village.

At 536 m the Col de Teghime rides over the base of the mountain ridge that divides Cap Corse. There are marvellous views to the west over the gulf of St Florent and to the east over Bastia. It was the site of the last battle for the liberation of Corsica from the Germans in October 1943. Troops sent from North Africa to support the Corsican resistance fighters captured the pass. Bastia was threatened and the German navy withdrew. I would like to pretend that we enjoyed the famous view from this point but nobody can organise the weather. We had been blessed with endless sunshine around Cap Corse but as we climbed the pass swirling clouds closed in around the mountains and we descended to Bastia in streaming rain.

3

The Green Desert

EAST COAST

Edward Lear's description, 'the green desert', matches my first memory of driving down the east coast of Corsica in 1963. In 1868 Lear saw an abandoned coast with a few yellow-faced locals whose strength was sapped by the malarial mosquito. When we drove down the straight road from Bastia to Bonifacio, it was a depressing wilderness of salt-scrub and ragged groves of provençal cane rustling in the slight breeze coming off the sea. The mosquito had been exterminated by American troops in 1944. An air of lethargy persisted. It remained a road without life.

However, it was in the early 1960s that plans were being made to restore life and fertility to this coast which it had not enjoyed since it was colonised by the Greeks and the Romans. The east road remains one of the least attractive in the island but it passes at various points the remains of some of the most important episodes in Corsican history. The east coast also symbolises the new developments which point the way to Corsica's economic future and the problems of the island's changing identity. After centuries of stagnation the east coast is now setting the pace for the future.

The long history of Corsica before the beginning of the Christian era is still obscure. In the last twenty-five years archaeologists have made unexpected discoveries and laid down an outline of events, at moments in some detail. But remains and artefacts are not always as precise as written records and excavations have left a trail of speculation and debate. The complexity of Mediterranean history in the Graeco-Roman period makes the subject more difficult for the layman but Corsica became an important part of that intricate history. In the unending trading rivalries of the Mediterranean, Corsica's position and her ports

1 Pleasure boats moored in the old port, Bastia

2 Bustling food market, Place de l'Hôtel-de-Ville, Bastia

3 Statue of Napoleon, Place St-Nicholas, Bastia

4 The 12th-century Pisan church, La Canonica, with ruins of Roman Mariana in the foreground, Bastia

were the attraction and were to remain so until the end of the eighteenth century when she passed into the protective possession of France.

About 565 BC, a Greek colony in Phocaea, Asia Minor, were driven out by the Persians and, taking to their ships, arrived on the east coast of Corsica. Here they founded a new colony called Alalia, now known by its Roman name, Aleria. It had long been thought that there had been a Greek colony in Corsica but no remains had ever been discovered. The reason was simple. When the Romans built and expanded their town of Aleria, they obliterated the remains of the older Greek town on this site.

Aleria had long been recognised as some kind of Roman settlement. Even Prosper Mérimée, visiting Corsica in 1839 as a government inspector of historic monuments, knew of Aleria's existence, almost exactly 120 years before the first excavations. When the first systematic excavations began in 1955, the archaeologists thought that they were going to uncover a minor Roman trading port. They discovered that Aleria had been a town of some size and importance. More surprising, on the western outskirts of the Roman town they found a Greek necropolis. The range and quality of the objects found in the tombs, including ceramics dating from the sixth century BC, showed that this was the site of Alalia and that it had been a wealthy and important Greek trading colony.

The Phocaean Greeks had to defend their new settlement. Only twenty-five years after landing in Corsica, about 540 BC, they defeated a combined Etruscan and Carthaginian fleet in a sea battle just off Alalia. The large Etang de Diane immediately north of Alalia provided a fine natural harbour. From then on the many trading states and nations of the Mediterranean kept an envious eye on Alalia and, later, all the other ports in Corsica. We know almost nothing of the relations between the Greeks and the Corsican people who were living in a primitive stage of the Iron Age. One early source describes them as a peaceful, pastoral people who lived inland, tending their herds and leading an unusually law-abiding life.

The Greeks introduced olive trees, wheat and the vine into

Corsica. They found clay for their own pottery and mined copper, iron, lead and silver for their own use and for export. They also found the murex shellfish which produced the dye called Tyrrhenian purple, the colour so prized for fabrics in the classical world. The dye must have been their most important export.

It is the contents of the tombs, particularly the fine Greek ceramics, that confirm Alalia's importance, prosperity and wide trading contacts. There are not only Attic vases painted by well-known artists but dishes, wine cups and other ceramics from important Greek trading colonies in Sicily, Spain and France. The Phocaeans joined Corsica to the trading routes of the Mediterranean. After a time they moved their capital to Marseilles. Alalia became a staging post on the way to their new colony, Velia, in southern Italy. The Carthaginians occupied Alalia in 278 BC but lost the island to the Romans in 259 BC.

It took the Romans a hundred years to subdue the whole island but from that time to their departure around AD 550, Corsica enjoyed an unequalled period of peace and prosperity. The Romans built ports all round the island – Pliny lists twelve – and they developed the agriculture and fishing industry established by the Greeks. They brought irrigation to Corsica which made the east coast highly fertile. They introduced Latin and Roman law. And eventually they brought Christianity. From the fourth century bishoprics were created at Aleria, Mariana, Nebbio and Ajaccio. It was the foundation stone for the wider missionary activities of the Pisans in the medieval period.

The excavations at Aleria and the many artefacts discovered there prove that Corsica, linked with Sardinia, was a more important Roman colony than had previously been suspected. Corsica was so close to mainland Italy, one might have expected more comment from Roman writers in official documents about life in the colony and relations with the Corsican people. It is clear that the wealth Corsica produced was used according to changing imperial needs. There was probably some slavery but it is unlikely that many Corsicans were employed in official positions. The Romans built a few towns on the main rivers but made little attempt to settle the interior or to interfere with the traditional life and customs of the people. Apart from their mining activities, the Romans had little interest in the central mountains of Corsica.

The excavated ruins of Aleria are impressive but not beautiful. Apart from the remains of one arch, the site is a ground plan of low walls and stumps of pillars but none of the brick and stone remains is more than 1 m high. There are fragmentary remains of the main temple, a large forum with porticos and shops and, raised on a terrace, the praetorium with accompanying living rooms and baths. The governor lived in style and comfort, and ruled over a substantial town. Only the official area of Aleria has yet been excavated. The main town is still buried and one day may reveal more detail of Roman life in Corsica.

In the October sun the site looked dry and bleak. Aleria is situated on a hill set well back from the sea. Trees have been planted but they will give neither shade nor character to the site for several years. I wandered through the praetorium to the western edge of the hill. The steep slope must have provided the Romans with natural protection. Although nothing is marked the Greek necropolis must have been here on the upper slope of the hill. It was here that a small sound stirred my imagination and brought ancient Aleria alive. From the valley below came the soft, mellow note of the bells of a large herd of goats and sheep. The sound was as arcadian and evocative as pastoral poetry or the pipes of Pan. The herd spread across a large meadow to where the river meandered through lush woodland. I was looking over a fertile countryside that the Greeks and Romans had first created here and which centuries later was being restored by invaders of a different kind.

We had difficulty in finding the museum and the ruins. I thought the Roman town was close to the sea and at the crossroads turned left instead of right. A clear signpost to this major tourist attraction would have helped. We drove past a shuttered resort hotel and two deserted camping sites before I knew that I was not heading for Aleria. We turned back, drove over the main road and soon came to an enormous car park enclosed by a wire fence. There was no sign indicating the direction of the museum or the site. Up the hill a village was dominated by an impressive sixteenth-century Genoese fort which turned out to be the museum. Perhaps this anonymity is a security measure against vandals or site robbers. The system kept us perplexed for twenty-five minutes.

The Musée Jérôme Carcopino, named after the archaeologist and classical historian who stimulated interest in Aleria, is housed in the eleven small rooms on the ground floor of the newly restored Genoese fort. It is best to see the museum before visiting the excavations. The exhibits and the explanations in the museum will help you to understand the site. The interior of the building and the museum display are attractive though there is not enough space in these tiny rooms for this large collection of fine objects. It is overwhelming. The expert could find his way amongst this mass of material. A more selective and better labelled display would be more intelligible to the general public. The rooms are almost filled by large glass cases with shelf upon shelf of Greek ceramics, Roman pottery, fragments of glass, ivory, iron and bronze weapons, coins and a tomb complete with the manacled skeleton of a prisoner. Several of the Greek vases and wine cups are of the finest quality. The friezes of miniature painting present a masque of antique life and legend. The museum may leave you confused but it will leave you in no doubt that Aleria was an important and prosperous place in both Greek and Roman times.

Fifty-five kilometres up the coast, just south of Bastia's airport, are the fragmentary ruins of Mariana, the other important Roman town and port on the east coast. In 93 BC, Marius established a new Roman settlement here, populated it is said with veteran soldiers of his own campaigns. The Romans began to cultivate this plain of the Golo river and later a port was built. It became the Romans' main base in northern Corsica and, by the fourth century AD, an important centre of Christianity. Today, the small ruined area of brick walls shows the remains of houses, baths and the palaeo-Christian basilica and baptistry. The crumbling mosaics still contain a few recognisable Christian symbols. It is salutory and sad to see great endeavours reduced to a few dull walls of thin brick. But in the sixth century AD Corsica was invaded by the Vandals, the Ostrogoths and the Lombards. They pillaged and destroyed Aleria and Mariana. The fertile eastern plain between the Tavignano and the Golo rivers in time became waterlogged and infested by malarial mosquitoes. However, Mariana was to become the birthplace of Corsica's next period of civilisation. After the departure of the Romans, Corsica suffered a long dark age with six centuries of invasion and destruction. The Vandals ruled Corsica from AD 469 to 534. It was then absorbed into the Byzantine empire but suffered an invasion by the Ostrogoths in the middle of the sixth century. At the end of the sixth century Pope Gregory the Great encouraged missionary activity in the island but at about the same time the Lombards attacked and by 725 Corsica had become part of the Lombard kingdom of Italy. In the eighth century, through the influence of Charlemagne, the Pope assumed sovereignty over the island. But turbulence continued. From the eighth until the early eleventh century the Saracens raided the coast and controlled much of Corsica's coastal region. What influence these endless invasions had on the Corsican people one can only guess. From the arrival of the Greeks onwards some of the local people were made slaves. Later, many Corsicans were carried off by Barbary pirates into slavery in North Africa. A few of them, with Corsican energy and enterprise, obtained their freedom, organised the piracy and, in a few cases, became local potentates, returning to plunder their own homeland.

For centuries the Corsicans must have withdrawn to the comparative safety of the mountains and forged their own culture in that barren and unrelenting world where they learned to make survival their way of life and where in time they seemed to lose any ambition to improve their conditions. Recent influences are rapidly destroying the differences but when I first came to Corsica the coast and the mountains still seemed like different worlds. The larger ports such as Bastia had a certain Corsican sombreness but it was nothing to the sense of darkness, silence and introversion in Sartène and other places of the Corsican heartland. It struck one as a world without colour, without joy and without laughter. It was a character that is difficult to define but it gave the feeling of being exceedingly old. And this was in 1963 when Corsica was already waking up to the outside world and in reality much of the traditional way of life was dead or dying.

A few yards north of the ruins of the Roman city of Mariana stands a simple but beautiful romanesque church, Santa-Maria-Assunta (St Mary of the Assumption), now known usually as La Canonica. The name is thought to have referred originally to the canons of this cathedral. The church symbolises the long period when Corsica was under the protection of the archbishops of Pisa. By the early eleventh century the Saracens were retreating from Corsica and for about seventy years the island was ruled by local lords and elected chieftains, each administering their own regions. In 1077 Pope Gregory VII sent Landolphe, then Bishop of Pisa, to reassert papal authority over the local bishops and the seignorial rulers. In 1091, Pope Urban V gave the island as a fiefdom to Daibertus, later to become the first Archbishop of Pisa. The Pisans eventually lost Corsica to Genoa in 1284 but their period of rule is still commemorated by some 300 Pisan romanesque churches scattered all over the island. Many of them are in places which must have been remote when they were built and which lay hidden and unknown until recent years.

The Pisan efforts to reorganise and stimulate the church in Corsica show the missionary energy and zeal of medieval Christianity. They began by building churches around the coast, mostly near the sites of former Roman towns. Later, dividing the island into *pievi*, groups of villages and hamlets like the later cantons, no matter how remote, they provided each *pievi* with a church. This was built in a place central to the community it served and was accessible by existing tracks and paths.

When one considers the architectural and structural quality of even the simplest and most remote of these churches, the organisation is matched only by the act of faith. As a result of movements of population and extensive rebuilding during the sixteenth century, a great number of these churches lost their villages and hamlets and their congregations. Some have fallen into ruin, others are now isolated by the dense maquis. But some remain accessible and in good condition, from the grand, triple-naved basilicas such as La Canonica to the simplest, single-nave churches deep in the mountains.

The danger of enthusing about these churches is that it may cause others to be disappointed. Some might find them too austere, others monotonous but in different ways I was moved by all those that I saw. I remember walking through a quiet citrus grove to the south of La Canonica. I turned back and the church stood high above the trees and hedgerows. It was late afternoon and the mellow sunlight emphasised the variety of colour in the church's stonework, carefully chosen and cut by the Pisan masons. The plain walls with the narrow lancet windows dominated yet kept harmony with the surrounding countryside. But it would be wrong to over-emphasise the simplicity of these churches. Architecturally, they are really the most sophisticated in Corsica and, in many ways, the best built. La Canonica was completed in 1119. In recent times part of the upper south wall has been clumsily patched and the roof has been covered with modern tiles, but these disfigurements have not destroyed the perfect proportions of the church, the central nave rising above the two outer naves to lighten the main body of the structure. At the east end the small, projecting apse relieves the monotony of the main rectangular building while its slender pillars and the line of lancet windows provide enough features to enliven the structure. Examine the stonework and you will see how carefully variations in colour have been chosen and contrasted. The masons had few resources but they made the most of them and put them together with a standard of craftsmanship rare in Corsica.

These churches were the work of architects and stonemasons sent from Pisa. Although humble by contemporary Pisan standards and decorated only with small pieces of sculpture, they have the quality of the best romanesque tradition. It is extraordinary that one small Italian state could spare so much effort and expense to provide churches and an ecclesiastical organisation of such a high standard. The interiors of most of these churches are now ruined or derelict. They must have been impressive in their day and I like to imagine the scene at the consecration of La

Canonica in 1119 when the Bishop and attendant priests stood by the new altar, their colourful vestments contrasting with the simplicity of the pillared naves before them. The Pisans brought great gifts to Corsica. Her other invaders were more concerned with what they could take away.

I would add one word of caution. Everywhere you go in Corsica you will find these Pisan churches marked on your map or mentioned in the standard French guide-books. If you turn up each side road to visit them, it will take you a great deal of time and into some inaccessible places. I have chosen and described a few of the best which illustrate the different styles and features of these Corsican romanesque churches. That selection will be ample for most people. Anyone considering a deeper investigation of the subject will be on the back roads of Corsica for several months.

La Canonica moved me by its quiet simplicity and rural setting. In the fields sheep grazed. The silence was broken by the bleating of a stray lamb, answered by the guttural cries of the shepherd. There are animals of a more symbolic kind carved around the arch of the west door. Here, between a lion and a wolf the lamb carries a cross. On the lintel above the door is a running pattern of leaves. On the battered wooden west doors there was a modern and striking poster for a local dance. This suggests a continuing and lively parish life but the parishioners have long gone and the inside of the church is bare. Nothing is left except for the pleasing proportions of the three naves.

Nearby, and slightly difficult to find, is a smaller but older Pisan church, San Parteo. You cannot see it from La Canonica. Return a few metres to the open area in front of the only café in that neighbourhood and drive down the rough track that runs to the south-west. San Parteo is about 300 km on the left-hand side.

A few remains have been found of an older church dating from the fifth century which was built over the body or the relics of St Parteo, a Corsican martyr. The Pisan church dates from the eleventh century although the single nave was reconstructed in the following century. The upper part of the church has been disfigured by an ugly restoration with concrete and orange tiles but the delicate, eleventh-century apse makes the visit worthwhile. Around the semicircular apse delicate columns of granite, taken from a classical building, support a light arcading. It is charming but despite its delicacy maintains a balance with the main church.

Above a door in the south wall is a lintel carved with two lions separated by a stylised tree, an old oriental motif which came into the repertoire of medieval ornament through eastern textiles. The stonework of San Parteo shares a feature with La Canonica and many later buildings in Corsica, religious and secular. The holes in the walls that held the scaffolding while the church was being erected were left unfilled to make an additional pattern on the walls. There may have been a practical as well as a decorative purpose. The stone blocks of the Pisan churches are most precisely cut, dressed and laid. Once the wall was finished there may have been no neat way of filling the small scaffolding holes without spoiling the near-perfect surface of these walls.

The east coast of Corsica and its hinterland saw the invasion and civilising influences of Greeks, Romans and Pisans. It also adjoins the area of the Castagniccia, the great chestnut forests, where Corsica's own life and culture reached their highest level of prosperity and a more civilised way of life. A hundred years ago this was the richest and the most populous area of Corsica. While not so prosperous today, it is still beautiful countryside, full of villages and hamlets which offer a glimpse of the past. The excursion takes about half a day. For interest and the loveliest countryside it is worth every minute. Unlike Cap Corse, la Castagniccia is at its best in the autumn when the chestnuts are fully grown but still on the tree.

On the main road running south from Bastia, where you may have turned left to Mariana, now turn right following the signposts to Ponte Leccia. Here, follow the signs to Morosaglia, turning back eastwards to drive through la Castagniccia on narrow, winding roads which lead through the hills and mountains of this area. It is about 90 km back to the coast but it is a slow road and there are several places where it is worth stopping for interest or simply to enjoy the view.

Shortly after you have turned back east at Ponte Leccia, the chestnut forest begins. You enter a venerable and green-shaded world. Indeed, these huge trees – many 20 m high, the main trunks 2 m in diameter – appear so ancient that one feels one is travelling through an indigenous, almost primeval Corsican landscape. Nothing could be further from the truth. These chestnut trees were carefully planted and cultivated from the sixteenth century onwards with the encouragement of the Genoese. They were motivated by economic self-interest although it also brought prosperity to this area.

The Genoese wanted to encourage agriculture in Corsica. They failed in the south-eastern half of the island. This was the granite Dila dai Monti where the people clung to their independent and traditional ways. The north-eastern half of Corsica, the Diqua dai Monti, the schist region, was naturally more fertile. Here, with stick and carrot methods, the Genoese were more successful and the cultivation of wheat, barley, oil and wine increased. But the Genoese needed the grain for home consumption and it was necessary to find a substitute for the Corsicans. Flour produced from chestnuts provided the answer. From the sixteenth to the nineteenth centuries chestnut forests were planted where the indigenous oak had grown before and the most important of these forests was la Castagniccia. The chestnut was called 'the tree of bread' and the area became the most prosperous in Corsica.

The chestnut forest and the flour it produced led to the development of a distinct local culture, from crafts to cooking and, more important, a taste for politics. I was tantalised to read in one book that at a local wedding in this district, known for its elaborate cooking, as many as twenty dishes using chestnut flour might once have been served at the bridal feast. Today, driving the length and breadth of Corsica, the tourist will find it difficult to discover twenty-two genuine Corsican dishes of any kind and few would contain chestnut flour. No doubt several of the traditional dishes are still made in people's homes but few are served in restaurants.

The higher standard of living in la Castagniccia encouraged

the growth of craftsmanship and some artistry, noticeably lacking elsewhere in Corsica, particularly in the south where the austere way of life seems to have deprived the people of any visual sense. In la Castagniccia the chestnut wood was used for building and making furniture. There were skilled blacksmiths and cutlers and the best gunsmiths in the island; a fact noted by James Boswell who was impressed by the quality of the local weapons. There were skilled chair-makers, shoemakers, basketmakers and craftsmen who fashioned briar pipes. More unusual in Corsica, several of the churches have attractive wall-paintings by local artists.

The chestnut forests are beautiful. There are strong contrasts of sunlight and shadow among the deep vistas between the huge trees. Where the sun strikes the spreading branches their fruit is a brilliant green. The prickles of each husk sparkle like an aureole. The valleys fall away from the road on the left. Where the forest stretches down the slopes there is a sombre silence in the shade between the gnarled trunks brightened occasionally by clumps of yellow flowers or, more delicate, the miniature, pink autumn cyclamen scattered across the ground. Along the roadside fat, mottled sows and scatterbrained piglets rootle among the leaves for the first fallen chestnuts. The older pigs look sly and self-concerned as they gorge their way to the butcher's table. They have long been an important additional product of the chestnut forest.

The road winds on, the valleys to the left, the slopes of Monte San Petrone rising sharply on the right. The chestnut trees like an altitude between 400 and 800 m and where the road rises higher you lose them. From higher ground or when there is a break in the forest, there are frequent views to old villages and hamlets far below the road. On a ridge of land or climbing the slope of the valley, the stone houses cluster around the church and its bell-tower, riding the green waves of the great forest that encircles them. The number of the villages and hamlets indicates the past prosperity of la Castagniccia. Its wealth has long gone but its beauty remains.

The Genoese were responsible for the creation of this peaceful, once prosperous region but ironically la Castagniccia fostered

Corsicans with a new spirit of independence. By the eighteenth century the region had become the cradle of Corsican insurgence. When you turn east from Ponte Leccia, the first canton you come to is Morosaglia. The village is on the side of a hill looking over the chestnut forest and away to the fierce mountains of the Niolo. In a hamlet just beyond the main village, Pasquale Paoli was born. He was to become the greatest leader in Corsica's struggle for independence. The small house is now a museum. There are portraits and relics of the Paoli family and, on the ground floor, a chapel containing the remains of Pasquale. He ended his life in exile in London. In 1889 his remains were brought back to this remote village from St Pancras cemetery. Exile has been the fate of Corsica's most famous men, on whichever side they fought.

The Paoli family were typical of the prosperous men of la Castagniccia who were determined to fight for the independence of Corsica, freeing it from the rule of Genoa or any imposed allegiance to other European powers. A national rebellion broke out in 1729 near Corte and immediately autonomists rose up in arms all over the island. A constitution was declared at Corte in January 1731 and Giacinto Paoli, father of the family, was made one of the three governors of the new nation. The Genoese sought the help of the French, who had their own plans to take over the island. French troops defeated the rebels in 1739 and Giacinto Paoli went into exile with his younger son, Pasquale. They settled in Naples.

Pasquale was fourteen and his exile in Naples, first at school and afterwards at university, gave him a sound education he could not have received at home. He spoke and wrote Latin, Italian, French and English. His reading ranged from Plutarch to Montesquieu. He told Boswell that he had learnt his English from a group of Irishmen serving in Naples. Boswell was 'diverted with his English library' which included Pope's *Essay on Man* and Swift's *Gulliver's Travels*. Pasquale was naturally gifted but his exile in Naples strengthened his intellect and developed his advanced ideas on liberal government. They also turned this boy from an obscure Corsican village into a highly educated and civilised man who could hold his own in any company in Europe.

The full story of Paoli's fight for independence centres on his declared capital of Corte and I shall save it until we reach that town. But it was the men of la Castagniccia who first inspired the movement and although the Paolis, father and son, became the leaders, much of their support came from their neighbours. Among these were the Franciscan friars with some large friaries in la Castagniccia. They were to give strong moral support to the struggle for independence in a number of different ways.

Follow the road as it twists through the forest, watching out for the spotted pigs by the roadside and soft-eyed cows reclining in the middle of the road always, it seemed, immediately after the sharpest bends. Just before the turning to Orezza, whose spring produces the only mineral water in Corsica, to the left a towering ruined church rises up out of the forest. This was the friary of Orezza where in April 1731 twenty clergy debated solemnly the morality of the revolt against the Genoese. The Corsican rebels were good Catholics. The vague resolution of the conference left everyone's conscience unbruised. This friary later witnessed a famous mission by a holy friar preaching against the evil of the vendetta. In 1790 Paoli and Napoleon held a meeting here. The Franciscans left after the French Revolution and the roof of their great church collapsed in 1934. The church was further damaged by the Germans in September 1943.

Today, little remains of the friary. The church is roofless and to one side stands the decapitated campanile; the truncated upper storey rises out of an encroaching mesh of ivy. The walls of the tall nave lean precariously inwards. A notice forbids you to enter. It is good advice but the surrealist spectacle of disintegrating stuccoed altars and fragments of wall paintings emerging from the undergrowth is irresistible. Beyond the brambles mixed with maquis and wild flowers, pilasters and ornate corinthian capitals crumble in the shade of sprawling fig trees. The best-preserved altar with considerable painted decoration lay behind an impenetrable thicket. For fifteen minutes I struggled to get near enough to take some photographs but I was defeated. The decaying church had an atmosphere which was somehow exotic and tropical. It reminded me of the collapsed missionary churches of Antigua in Guatemala. But there the ruins had turned to wild gardens, the ragged walls, tumbled by earthquakes, softened by cascades of bougainvillea and deep blue morning glory. The crumbling stonework of Orezza is a wilderness and before long the top-heavy walls will collapse into the waiting maquis. The friars' memorial will be no more than a heap of rubble.

Neither in la Castagniccia nor anywhere else in the island where there are chestnut forests did we see any signs of serious harvesting. I could not find any place where the flour is still made nor was it for sale in the shops selling Corsican food. Everywhere the pigs were allowed to roam free and no doubt have always been the scavengers of these forests. Chestnut flour must still be made somewhere for it is an essential ingredient in certain Corsican dishes and in some places you can buy sweet cakes made from the flour, the cake baked on a chestnut leaf like the ricepaper of a macaroon. But the production must be small compared to the days when it made la Castagniccia the richest area in Corsica. But recalling the crude wooden instruments for producing the flour which we saw in the museum at Bastia, it must have been laborious work requiring a labour force which has long deserted those picturesque villages amidst the forest.

Out of la Castagniccia and down the precipitous road back to the coastal plain. In a few kilometres we drive from the prosperity of the past into an area which symbolises Corsica's new development and growing wealth. What the Greeks, the Romans and the Pisans achieved on the east coast is impressive. What the new invaders of this region have done in the last quarter of a century is a distinct transformation. It is not only the speed at which it has been achieved but the deep effect it is having on the whole life of Corsica; upheavals and changes so deep that they are still beyond calculation.

1954 was the year that marked the beginning of the end of the French empire. It was the year of the disaster of Dien Bien Phu and the beginning of the revolt in Algiers. French Indo-China was lost and by 1962 Algeria was independent. Enormous numbers of French colonists, many born in the colonies, returned to

France to find work and to settle to a new way of life.

Among them were a large number of Corsicans. For years, even centuries, lack of opportunity at home had driven Corsicans to emigrate all over the world, many of them successful colonists in the French empire. The exact figures can never be calculated but it has been estimated that there were some 100,000 Corsicans in North Africa and possibly another 12,000 in the Far East. A great many of these displaced Corsicans decided to return to their island. The emigration began in the early sixties and with the Corsicans came other French colonists and a considerable Arab workforce.

At the same time, in 1960, the French government and the local authorities in Corsica launched a scheme to improve the island's economy by increasing and modernising its agriculture. The basic problem for most Corsican farmers was a lack of capital together, no doubt, with an unwillingness to try new methods. The authorities created an organisation named SOMIVAC which, through research and finance, was to open up new farming land which was to be parcelled out to the island's farmers.

At this moment the French colonists started to arrive in Corsica, eager to find farming land and, unlike the local farmers, equipped with capital and modern expertise. The problem was made worse since there was only one large area in Corsica which could be developed, the east coastal plain. This had long been known in Corsica as the 'Lost Eldorado', a name based on the legend of the fertility and wealth created here by the Romans. Today, it might be called the 'New Eldorado', doubly enriched by the successful farming and wine growing of the ex-colonists and their entrepreneurial skills which have developed a successful tourist industry. They have achieved similar success elsewhere in the island if not on such a spectacular scale. They are also established in the commercial life of Ajaccio and Bastia. There must be many Corsicans who are either jealous of their success or, more important, dislike the way that they are destroying the traditional life of the island; not least by encouraging a vast invasion of tourists into the island each summer.

One might think that most Corsicans would be grateful to all these new invaders for creating wealth and jobs, the two things that the island has needed for centuries. But during those centuries the Corsicans developed an indifference to wealth and a dislike of work. Today, almost wherever you see men doing hard work, in the fields or in the restaurant kitchens, they are probably Arabs. All over Corsica I saw groups of men repairing the roads. There was always one man, presumably the foreman, sitting on the verge. He was a Corsican. The men digging were Arabs.

All over France the colonists who returned from North Africa are called 'les pieds-noirs' – the black feet. According to the dictionary this phrase simply means a Frenchman born in Algeria but sometimes I feel I hear Frenchmen use the phrase with pejorative overtones. Such nuances are difficult for the outsider to detect. I asked an English neighbour married to a 'pied-noir' farmer if she knew the origin of the phrase. According to her, when the French first settled in Algeria the Arabs had not seen men wearing boots or shoes before and they called the Frenchmen 'les pied-noids', referring to their black boots. She assured me that it was now nothing more than an amicable nickname. I doubt if that is always true and certainly not in Corsica. The graffiti on many Corsican walls make that plain.

Since Corsica was declared an integral part of France in 1789, too little has been done by the central government to solve the problems of the island. Napoleon was neglectful of his birthplace and did little to improve the economy of the island. During the nineteenth century roads and the railway were constructed and schools were built. Otherwise, the island was left to stagnate in its traditional poverty and thousands of Corsicans were forced to emigrate to find work. All this time the desire for independence smouldered away although it was not until the 1960s that the French government realised that some attempt had to be made to solve the problem.

Corsica's new prosperity stirred up new political activity in the island. The improved economy once again made an independent government seem a possibility and friction and jealousy between the new entrepreneurs and the traditionalists stimulated both moderate autonomists and the extreme *séparatistes* who rob banks

5 Quiet quayside at Centuri-Port, Cap Corse

6 The small port of Pino, Cap Corse

7 Intricately woven fishing traps, Cap Corse

8 A fisherman making new traps, Cap Corse

and plant bombs to achieve their ends. Like all political situations, it is extremely complicated and it is not easy to see where the moderates turn into the extremists. In 1970 the French government responded to the general political mood of Corsica and made it a separate region. More important, in 1982 a Regional Assembly was established, elected by universal suffrage in Corsica. This is not independence but it is the first region in France to have its own powerful local assembly.

There are many moderate Corsicans who are now more or less satisfied with this amount of autonomy and the possession of their own assembly no doubt gives a local spice to the endless political café debates. The official autonomist party has made good progress and by the democratic process has gained eight out of sixty-one seats and 20 per cent of the total vote. The members of the party are mainly young and left-wing but they have not joined forces with the communists.

Corsica remains a secretive place and it is difficult to get reliable information about the *séparatistes* who use the methods of terrorism to fight for the complete independence of Corsica. They have been known to rob four banks in one day in Ajaccio and there have been frequent bombings of public buildings and, as a gesture against tourism, a number of hotels. They claim that they try to avoid killing people but from time to time they bomb buildings which were not, as they thought, unoccupied. There is a considerable amount of fringe activity all over the island, walls disfigured by political outcries, and about 90 per cent of the signposts daubed with black paint and a large number pierced with bullet holes. Either way, many of them are now illegible and can make problems on remote routes.

One French journalist to whom I talked seemed to me to come nearest to the truth. 'The general opinion', he said 'is that there are probably only about two hundred active terrorists. But it has proved impossible to catch them. In the old days the ordinary person did not like the violence and the killings of the vendetta and the banditry but they would never give information to the authorities. These men may have been murderers but, more important, they were Corsicans. The same lingering code of honour protects the extremists. Nobody likes or approves of bombs but they are thrown by Corsicans. And under the same cloak of secrecy it is impossible to tell where the democratically elected autonomists end and the extremists begin. Some people suspect that somewhere the extremists are dovetailed into the formal political party. That is just another Corsican secret.'

The battle goes on, within and without the assembly although in a sense the true battlefield is the rich plain of the east coast. The problems and the deep-seated rivalries have not been solved. In the 1950s Corsicans accounted for 80 per cent of the population. Today, non-Corsicans must be nearing 45 per cent of the population with a far higher percentage control of the island's resources. The French government have made concessions to the traditionalists. The Corsican language is being taught in schools. Paoli's university in Corte has been re-established with a department devoted to Corsican studies. An enormous national park has been set up to protect the centre of the island and there are more local schemes to revitalise the rural areas. But there is a contradiction in all this activity. Any survival of any form of traditional life must depend on the sound economy being created by 'pied-noir' farming methods and their successful promotion of the island's tourist industry. It is this same new prosperity, attacked by the extremists, that offers Corsica its only hope of achieving further independence. An independent Corsica might see the east coast 'Eldorado' turn once again to a stagnant green desert. It is hard to believe that the majority of Corsica's population will allow the clock to be put back by a handful of extremists.

4

The First Citadel

BONIFACIO

The port of Bonifacio is at the extreme southern tip of Corsica, only 19 km from Sardinia. It has been known for centuries as one of the safest natural harbours in the Mediterranean and it is one of the most spectacular places in the island. The Genoese built their first citadel here but the history of Bonifacio goes back to far older times. This perfect and central haven must have been known to the Mediterranean's earliest mariners.

Those who believe that Homer set Odysseus' adventures in real places claim that Bonifacio was the setting for the terrible encounter with the Laestrygonians. The evidence is most convincing since the place and the surroundings described by Homer fit Bonifacio to the last detail. When Odysseus arrives, he finds 'an excellent harbour, closed in on all sides by an unbroken ring of precipitous cliffs, with two bold headlands facing each other at the mouth so as to leave only a narrow channel in between'. Climbing the cliffs, Odysseus looks over a hinterland described almost as it is today: 'No ploughed field or other signs of human activities were to be seen: all we caught sight of was a wisp of smoke rising up from the countryside.' Experts say that Corsica was known to Mycenaean seamen. One only hopes that the primitive inhabitants living around Bonifacio were not quite as terrifying as the cannibalistic Laestrygonians who *welcomed* Odysseus' companions to supper.

Legend has continued to combine with history to provide a notable list of visitors to this place of refuge from the sudden storms of the Mediterranean. It is said that St Helena came here and expressed her gratitude by giving the town a piece of the true cross. Whatever it is and however it came here, it remains the most precious relic of Bonifacio. Cynics may say that there are sufficient pieces of the true cross in churches around the world to reconstruct dozens of crosses but with such relics, faith cannot be quantified. The faithful also claim that St Francis of Assissi took refuge here while travelling from Italy to Spain in 1215 and founded the friary of St Julien but there is no real evidence for his visit. It is true that two of Corsica's nine original Franciscan friaries were founded in Bonifacio not so long after St Francis's supposed visit and it could be that this strong Franciscan presence gave rise to the legend.

There is no doubt that the Emperor Charles V spent a few days in Bonifacio in 1541 while in 1793, Napoleon, then an artillery officer, stayed for several months in Bonifacio preparing an expedition to Sardinia. A plaque marks the house where he stayed in the old town. Today, while the visitors to Bonifacio are less illustrious, they are far more numerous. It has become one of Corsica's main attractions helped by the fact that the fast road down the east coast makes it accessible in a one-day tour from many other resorts on the island.

The old town and the citadel are surprisingly unspoilt by the growth of tourism but the port has been more vulgarised than any other seaside resort in Corsica. Tourists must be catered for but the damage in Bonifacio comes from the lack of any planning or control. The main end of the harbour has sprawled into an untidy car park, spoiling one of the most enjoyable views of the port. As you stand in the car park getting your first view of Bonifacio and the old quay, it is not the prospect of the citadel that commands attention but a large and ramshackle floating restaurant; more like a disintegrating warehouse supported on a badly constructed raft. Since within 200 m of it there are at least twenty proper restaurants, offering menus at a variety of prices, one cannot see why the main view of the old quay should be blocked by this ark. It was closed in October so I cannot comment on its gastronomic importance. But it is all the more unnecessary since obviously it serves meals for only two or three months in the year.

I write with feeling since twenty-five years ago Bonifacio was a quiet and enchanting fishing port. Even then there were several small hotels and restaurants in the houses along the quay but they were less obtrusive and they had not covered the quayside with plastic chairs and tables and hoardings advertising milk shakes and hotdogs. There was plenty of life but it belonged to Bonifacio. Now the harbour is choked by a large floating marina and a variety of expensive yachts and below the walls of the citadel is a new jetty for the smart car-ferry to Sardinia. In 1963 our Mini was winched aboard a medium-sized fishing boat for the short crossing to Santa Teresa. All around us were fishing boats, large and small, and lobsters were so much cheaper then.

But nothing can ever spoil the extraordinary situation of this harbour locked within the security of its towering limestone cliffs and watched over by the Genoese citadel. Approaching from the sea one is faced with a line of striated cliffs, a mingling of white and tawny stripes with hanging patches of greenery and weed. At this point one can see part of the walls of the citadel and, built to the very edge of the precipitous cliffs, the tall houses of the old town. Wind and water have undercut the soft limestone leaving a sensational view of these topheavy houses perched on an overhanging crust of rock seeming to defy all the laws of nature. The sea laps greedily at the rocks far below, seeming to wait like some predator for the inevitable collapse. Something of this view can be seen from the land but the most dramatic views are seen from a boat.

Looking towards the land, to the west of the citadel there is an opening in the cliffs with a lighthouse to the left and the outer ramparts commanding the mouth of the port high on the right. Entering this mouth you keep straight ahead for about 300 m then turning left follow the channel for one kilometre where it brings you into the old fishing harbour. The harbour and the channel are formed and protected by a great spur of limestone rock which runs parallel to the main coast and is joined to it at the east end. At its widest the channel is hardly 200 m but the water is deep enough to allow the passage of quite large boats. In earlier times it could provide anchorage for a considerable fleet and protection during the most violent storms.

The town of Bonifacio is divided into three sections. Below is the old port, roughly pear-shaped and with buildings on the two facing quays, the buildings on the south side reaching to the foot of the citadel. A steep ramp leads up into the citadel and through a fortified gateway into the narrow streets of the old town. Beyond the town is a huge and desolate area, partly a military base, partly wasteland scattered with the remains of derelict old buildings and towards the end of the escarpment a huge cemetery surrounded by more modern fortifications and gun emplacements. It is a strange mixture and a brief account of its history is necessary before a tour of the town.

The best clue to Bonifacio's history and the nature of its people lies in its name. It was founded as a Genoese town by Genoese people and basically that it is how it has remained – more Italian than Corsican – with a language that owes more to Genoa than to Corsica or France. Throughout all Corsica's struggles for independence, Bonifacio, even more than Calvi, remained loyal to Genoa, a loyalty for which they paid a high price on occasions. The old Bonifacio lives on almost in secret in the shadows of the citadel walls and the alleys that run in a maze across the small town.

The early history of Bonifacio reads more like a great historical novel, heroic yet always sombre. The Romans almost certainly had a colony here but any trace of them was destroyed by later invaders. Known formerly as Giola, for centuries it must have been a haunt of pirates and other marauders. In 828, Count Bonifacio, returning from a successful campaign against the Saracens in North Africa, captured the peninsula, built a castle on it and gave the place his own name. During the twelfth century the Pisans and the Genoese pressed to gain possession of Bonifacio but in 1205 it finally passed into the hands of the Genoese.

The Genoese disposed of the inhabitants of the town and brought in their own colonists; some volunteers but mostly serfs who were paid to settle here. Bonifacio became almost a small, autonomous republic with its own senate and courts and important exemptions from taxes and customs duties which fostered the town's trading activities between Corsica, Sardinia and the mainland with some piracy on the side. They produced little themselves since the Corsicans did not allow them to develop the neighbouring land but it was a mercantile town and they made a good living from their trading.

Life can never have been easy for the small population of this isolated outpost but there were moments when their normal courage was further tempered by the horrors of plague and siege, both made more fearful by the confined nature of the small town. Their successful resistance to the long siege of 1420 says much for the townspeople's spirit and the fortifications of the Genoese citadel, the biggest that they built in Corsica; larger than Calvi and with a more elaborate system of defence. Impregnable from the sea, the towering walls and towers made it invincible from the land.

The citadel remains an impressive sight seen rising beyond the old fishing port, the hard outlines of its walls sharp against the sky. But how Edward Lear exaggerates the scene. By a coincidence, as I was writing, suddenly Lear's illustration of the 'Port of Bonifacio' was side by side on my desk with my own photograph of the same view taken from the identical spot where Lear must have stood and sketched. It is surprising how much can be matched exactly; the clustered masts of his fishing fleet are exchanged for the masts of the pleasure boats on the marina but the main outlines of the old port, the citadel and the cliffs enclosing the channel are the same. But by strong contrasts of black and white and by raising the bastions and ramparts of the citadel almost into the sky, Lear has given the scene a Dantesque drama that it does not in reality possess. It is a splendid prospect but not an Olympian one. Perhaps the lack of colour urged Lear into such exaggerations which *heighten* so many of the illustrations in his book.

But in August 1420, when Alfonso V of Aragon stood on the deck of his flagship, surrounded by his eighty invading ships in the channel below the ramparts of Bonifacio, the Genoese citadel may have appeared like a great castle in the sky. The siege had begun and the Spanish king, having just captured Calvi, thought he would have little difficulty in taking Bonifacio. Corsica was now almost in the grasp of this young, ambitious Spaniard and in his general strategy only Bonifacio now stood between him and the conquest of Sardinia, Sicily and the Republic of Genoa. Over the next few months he was to learn that he had underrated the courage and determination of the men of Bonifacio and, even more, the women. But who could have believed that a few hundred people in an isolated garrison town could hold out for months against some of the best soldiers in Europe?

The ordeal of that cramped town between 13 August 1420 and the ending of the siege on 5 January 1421 is hard to imagine. The citizens of Bonifacio had no firearms. For the best part of five months they were bombarded by Spanish guns placed on the opposite shore and picked off by musket-fire. They had limited supplies of food and water and by the third month those still alive were starving. Their resistance was sustained by the indomitable spirit of the women who fought alongside the men and before long outnumbered them. Conditions in the town must have been appalling and it was doomed unless help arrived from Genoa.

During the third month the town made a temporary truce with the Aragonese. They gave the Spaniards thirty-two child hostages and an undertaking to surrender at the end of forty days if no help had arrived from Genoa. In desperation the citizens built a small boat in the town and lowered it down the cliffside into the sea to race with a message for help to Genoa. Shortly before the truce expired a message came back that a Genoese fleet was on its way and should reach Bonifacio at any moment. The prayers and religious processions continued day and night, the Genoese fleet did not appear and the forty days ran out. King Alfonso demanded entry to the citadel.

The citizens debated between surrender and suicide. They knew that the Genoese fleet must be near, delayed only by unfavourable winds, and that a few more hours might save them. In the middle of the following night all the church bells suddenly started to ring and there was the sound of shouting and cheering. In the first light of dawn the Aragonese looked up at the ramparts and saw a large troop of Genoese soldiers marching in formation around the walls. It was the citizens' last desperate bluff to gain time. Every able-bodied man and woman, and there were more women than men, had dressed in the armour of the dead and formed a ghost army to deceive the Aragonese into thinking that help had arrived. The deception gained the necessary time and on Christmas Day the Genoese fleet appeared and after fierce fighting, aided by the remaining townspeople, they forced their way into the harbour and the Aragonese fleet retreated and sailed away, carrying the wretched child hostages with them. It was an important victory for the Genoese and in a few years they had reasserted their sovereignty throughout the island.

About one hundred years later disaster again struck Bonifacio. In 1528 the town was swept by the plague which killed two-thirds of the population. They can hardly have recovered from this disaster when in 1553 the town was once again under siege. This time it was the troops of Henry II of France supported by the fleet of the Turkish pirate, Dragut. The citadel was bombarded for eighteen days and nights. At dawn on the eighteenth day the men, women and children of Bonifacio fought off three successive assaults against the town. They fought with such determination and ferocity that Dragut was on the point of raising the siege and leaving.

At that moment Dominique Cattaciolo was caught returning from Genoa with a large sum of money intended to encourage the Bonifaceans to continue their resistance to the Franco-Turkish attack. Cattaciolo, probably to save his life, changed sides and Dragut saw how he could be used to trick the town into surrender. Cattaciolo appeared before the town council with a forged letter from the Genoese authorities stating that they were unable to help raise the siege. He also assured his fellow townsmen that if they surrendered, Dragut would spare their lives and their possessions. The Bonifaceans accepted the situation but hardly had they opened the citadel gates than the foreign troops poured in to massacre and pillage without mercy. They withdrew only under pressure from the Corsican leader, Sampiero, and a large payment of money but by that time once again the town had suffered terrible casualties and a great deal of damage. The citadel still stands solid against the sky, a memorial to these horrifying events. They read more like grand opera or a novel by

Victor Hugo than pages in the history of a town now invaded merely by international tourism.

The view of the harbour and the channel leading out to sea remain impressive and beautiful. Looking westwards, towards the rising battlements of the citadel, the tall houses lean over the quay and ragged cliffs rise behind them, sharp white limestone mixed with patches of rough turf. The best view of the old port is from the heights of the citadel, an aerial view of stepped orange-tiled roofs, white houses and white boats with blue water all around and the green, savage hinterland disappearing into the distance. There is now a new quay for the Sardinian steamers and a new customs house to match. In the nineteenth century Corsican and Sardinian bandits, wanted by the law, came in and out of Bonifacio concealed in small fishing boats. It might be more difficult now, not least because there are few fishing boats.

You climb to the citadel by a steep ramp arriving at an impressive gateway equipped with the old machinery for a drawbridge and portcullis. These fortifications look medieval but the Porte de Gênes was built in 1598 and was the only entrance to the citadel until a road was constructed up to the town and the Porte de France built in 1854. For the most part the old town has resisted the invasion of the tourist. There are cafés, restaurants, small nightspots offering the local guitar music and plenty of souvenir shops but they have all been fitted into the old buildings without changing or spoiling them or the atmosphere of the narrow streets and alleyways, prised apart by archways and flying buttresses.

The town is more for wandering than for sightseeing. One can see the houses where Charles V and Napoleon stayed in the rue des Empereurs and one can walk along a section of the walls. In the centre of the town is the main church, Ste-Marie Majeure with a large loggia spreading over the small square in front of it. The church has been altered a number of times and is not of distinction or interest except that it is here that the relic of the true cross is kept and this church has always been the centre of the town's life in moments of tragedy and celebration. Below the loggia and the square is an underground cistern where the winter rainfall was stored to sustain the town during the dry months. The loggia was also the place where the rulers of the town held public audience.

It is hard to believe that so much history has been enacted in this minute town which barely measures more than 150 m across its length and breadth. The tall houses, with their steep front steps, are crowded together in narrow alleys so that it is impossible to separate one building from another and even the churches disappear into the surrounding houses. Here and there the escutcheons of noble Genoese families are carved over the doorways of more substantial houses and along the southern edge of the town the darkness of the alleys gives way to the bright view of the sea. Here, built against the sheer cliff a precarious stairway runs from the town to the sea. It is called l'escalier du roi d'Aragon and one legend tells that it was built by the Spanish to break the siege. Quite how Spanish soldiers could have built 187 steps at this point without being seen by the townsfolk the legend does not explain. It must have been built by the Genoese themselves as their lifeline with the outside world and this was probably where their boat was lowered into the sea and speeded on its way to seek help from Genoa.

Walking westwards one emerges from the claustrophobic atmosphere of the old town onto an open limestone plateau which stretches out to the mouth of the harbour channel. This much larger area was the main area of the citadel and the first half of it is still occupied by a large army barracks. When I first came here the citadel had become the headquarters of the French Foreign Legion, recently forced to leave Algeria, and the whole of this area was closed to the public. Now the barracks are occupied by a commando unit and apart from the barracks one is free to wander all over this derelict and fascinating area. Just above the road leading to the barracks is a monument to the memory of the Legionnaires who gave their lives in a late nineteenth-century Algerian campaign. The Legion brought the monument with them and presented it to Bonifacio in 1963 when they established their garrison here. The heroic bronze statue – the soldier holding aloft the colours with one hand while staunching the mortal wound with the other – recaptures all the melodrama of *Beau Geste*, kepi and all.

There are two old churches in this area. To the south of the barracks is the plain but impressive small church of Saint Dominique, said to have been built in 1270 by the Templars returning from the Fourth Crusade and given to the Dominicans in 1307. It is possible that it was first built by the Dominicans as part of the neighbouring friary. The interior of the church was redecorated in the Genoese baroque style and the whole church has recently been restored. At first sight it appears to be within the confines of the barracks but the road leading to it is open to the public.

Beyond the barracks lies a wasteland of semi-ruined defensive towers, old windmills, crumbling barracks, the shells of unidentifiable buildings and a walled cemetery, all scattered over an area of white limestone rocks and patches of weed, thistle and occasional clumps of wildflowers which bring touches of colour to this brown and grey desolation. To one side of the cemetery are the forlorn remains of the Franciscan friary and church whose interior is now more like a tumbledown warehouse, ragged limestone walls and a rough floor where the weeds are rapidly encroaching. The sour smell of nettles has replaced the odour of sanctity. I wondered if the remains of Bishop Rafael Spinola had been left undisturbed since his burial here in the fifteenth century. He had requested that he be buried under the nave of this church so that his remains might be walked on by all who entered here. In his most profound humility I doubt if he can have envisaged this present penury where, sadly, few people walk at all. And that is partly the fault of the modern standard guide-books which give little attention to this part of the citadel. As I found the whole area fascinating I was frustrated by the lack of information. It has become a ghost town but history is made of ghosts.

There were many in Bonifacio who did not share Bishop Spinola's humble attitude in death. The large cemetery is more a city of the dead with its streets and squares. Each is lined with vaults and tombs in a great variety of architectural styles; in many cases, *fantasies* might be a more appropriate word. The small, and not so small, houses of the dead range from rustic hermitage through Gothic confectionery to neo-classic solemnity. Only members of the French Foreign Legion, in an obscure corner, were buried with decent simplicity. Strangely, the whole place was rather jolly, except for a cross-eyed, lame attendant who kept suspicious eyes on us. Many of the tombs would not have been out of place as exotic follies in an English eighteenth-century landscape garden. Indeed, several of them reminded me of those whimsical designs published in the eighteenth century by Mr Halfpenny, his name as improbable as his lathe-and-plaster architecture. I wonder if there were pattern books from which the bereaved might make their choice, altering a few details to make their tomb different or, more simply, a bit cheaper.

Back in the old port of Bonifacio you will have no difficulty in finding a boat to take you out to view the town from the sea and to visit a few local grottoes. The ticket touts have become a nuisance and the kiosks selling tickets along the quay are a further intrusion on the former view of the old port. But the excursion is rewarding. The views of the eroded cliffs and the precarious little town are magnificent and within the cliffs are some dramatic grottoes where tricks of light turn the sea to strange and brilliant colours. There is the grotte de St-Antoine and, most dramatic, the grotte du Sdragonato. Here, the roof of the grotto rises in a high dome which is pierced by a hole in the shape of Corsica illuminated by the sky beyond.

From Bonifacio there are one or two short excursions in the neighbourhood. One can visit the lighthouse of Pertusato with a panoramic view back to Bonifacio along the cliffs. There are beaches in the gulf of Sta Manza and on the way the ancient friary of St Julien where St Francis is said to have taken refuge. And if you can persuade a boatman to take you, there is the old Roman quarry on the little island of Cavallo, the last dressed stones lying where the slaves left them when the Romans abandoned the island.

On my second visit we spent only one night in Bonifacio. In a snobbish determination to avoid the tourism of the quayside we decided to stay the night at a hotel we had seen on the main road just outside the town. There was plenty of room but the manageress warned us that the hotel's restaurant had closed. We were not worried as we had seen a small restaurant open just along the road and there were many restaurants in Bonifacio.

When it was time for dinner we felt tired and it was pouring with rain. We decided to make a dash for the local restaurant up the road. A light was on but there was little other sign of life and no other diners. None of the tables was laid, there was no smell of cooking and the little restaurant had an abandoned air. We stood in the door reluctant to retreat into the rain. At that moment a thin, nervous man emerged from what appeared to be the kitchen, switched on a second dim light and offered us a table. He returned immediately to the kitchen where we could hear him in consultation with his wife. Had the whole room not been so threadbare and worn one might have felt that the elderly couple had entered the restaurant business that night and that we were their first customers. Everything was tentative, the service, the preparation of the meal and, when it came, the meal itself. The carafe of vin rosé was the only bad wine we had during our tour of Corsica.

But what am I complaining about? It was exactly like all the wine we drank in 1963. Nostalgia must accept the rough with the smooth. And throughout this grotesque meal I was haunted by the cruel fact that we could have been sitting down among the tourists enjoying memorable fish soup followed by local lobsters. But there was something endearing about the elderly man as he hobbled backwards and forwards from the kitchen with baskets of stale bread and other delicacies. One must be prepared to pay a small price for not going with the crowd.

5

Older Worlds

SARTÈNE

The small town of Sartène and the area around it is the heart of traditional Corsica. It has an early history and monuments dating back several thousand years and in much later times it was the centre of the Corsican vendetta and banditry and the home of a strange heresy. The darkest sides of the Corsican nature developed in this region which led to the acts of implacable vengeance and violence which has created the world's melodramatic view of the Corsicans.

We drove down from Ajaccio to the great Gulf of Valinco, intending to stay the night in Propriano which used to be a quiet fishing village with the shimmering sea stretching way across the gulf. The hotel I had enjoyed previously had closed for the winter and the former quay had turned into a 'strip' of crowded cafés, unwelcoming waiters and the local *jeunesse* shouting at their friends in passing cars. The line of small hotels looked scruffy and the place had lost all its appeal. The distant shore across the gulf looked deserted and inviting, if we could find a hotel. We took the risk and set off for Porto-Pollo on the extremity of the northern shore.

Once we were driving along the north of the gulf one could see that it was being developed as a summer resort but in October it was deserted, the few hotels closed and the camping sites empty. It was a fine stretch of coast with good beaches lining the gulf. Inland there was a gentle, rural scene of pasture and woodland stretching up the slope of the hill, a change from the more usual rugged scenery of Corsica. By the time we reached the hamlet of Porto-Pollo we had passed enough closed hotels to make us concerned although our *Michelin* assured us that an open hotel existed there. At the end of the road was a plain, stone building which declared itself a hotel although there was no sign of activity. The front door was open and we went into the lobby where we found the owners, mother and two daughters, sitting knitting. The old mother was a dark-faced crone in black and before giving us a key she impounded our passports. There was something conspiratorial about all three women and I was reminded of the Conrad hero who arrives at a remote hotel only to awaken in the middle of the night to see the four-poster bed slowly descending to suffocate him.

Le Golfe Hotel turned out to be a model of the best kind of simple French hotel, spotlessly clean, a shower that worked and, best of all, 100 m away and overlooking a small bay, a restaurant where we had an exceptionally good dinner and breakfast. I have no doubt that this stretch of coast will be developed further in the future although one could ask for nothing more than the existing comfort of Le Golfe Hotel and restaurant. Even the old lady in black became quite friendly once we were established.

We had not come to this neighbourhood to enjoy the sea air. Porto-Pollo was charming but nearby was Filitosa, the most extraordinary place in Corsica and one of the most haunting megalithic sites in Europe. The strange statues and structures of Filitosa are solid enough but their origins are obscure, still surrounded by academic speculation and debate. Since Filitosa dates back to the third millennium BC it is extraordinary how much has been discovered about its early inhabitants. It is even surprising that Filitosa was ever discovered at all and recognised as an elaborate prehistoric site. The statue-menhirs had been discovered – and misinterpreted – early in the nineteenth century. Prosper Mérimée attributed them to the Romans. Even quarter of a century ago, when I first visited Filitosa, Roger Grosjean, the French archaeologist, was still at work uncovering the site and interpreting his finds, a study he had begun in 1954.

Filitosa is hidden deep in the countryside. The narrow, rutted road winds up and down between fields and small thickets with outcrops of rock breaking through the turf. Cows and a few horses graze here and there and just when we thought we must have taken the wrong road we came on the hamlet of Filitosa.

Everything is better organised now. A pleasant café stands by the entrance to the site where you buy your tickets. A pathway leads downhill through old olives and an avenue of pines. Suddenly, there is a clearing and in the middle stands the most famous statue-menhir in Corsica – statue Filitosa V – the best preserved and armed with long-sword and dagger. The lines on the back of the figure suggest a cloak or similar clothing and the face, though only just emerging from the mass of the stone, is powerful and human. Apart from its intrinsic qualities the menhir is moving as one of European man's first moves to the art of sculpture and the representation of himself in stone.

The weapons carried by this figure pose one of the central problems of Filitosa and the megalithic culture of Corsica. They even create doubt about the identity of the figure itself. The site of Filitosa, which shows various stages of occupation, was probably first inhabited in the sixth millennium, a dating suggested by early neolithic ceramics found there. The megalithic civilisation was not established there until the beginning of the third millennium. This civilisation was characterised by the building of communal tombs called dolmens with massive slabs of stone raised on top of each other and the stone 'pillar-type' monuments called menhirs which later developed into portraits with a rough body-shape and simple facial features.

This megalithic civilisation had spread all over the Mediterranean and as far north as Scandinavia and Orkney. It includes such famous monuments as the circles of Stonehenge and Brodgar and the procession of figures at Carnac in Brittany. It has been suggested that this culture spread out from the eastern Mediterranean, possibly from Palestine, and that it involved a belief in a creative and destructive goddess who appears in different symbols. The elaborate burial chambers suggest a belief in some kind of immortality and the possibility that ancestors had the power of intercession with the creator.

This widespread megalithic culture was not, except in its cyclopean building, a uniform civilisation. It developed in different places at different times and, for example, the statue-menhirs became more developed in Corsica than anywhere else in Europe. We have little idea how the fundamental ideas were spread and how much influence one area had on another. Corsica was open to megalithic influences from France, Spain and elsewhere but the fact remains that the discovery and uncovering of Filitosa posed more questions than it answered.

I find the site of Filitosa a beautiful and haunting place. The megalithic settlement is spread over a wooded spur of rock which thrusts out above the green floor of a small valley shaded by scattered woodlands of old olives and holm-oaks. All over the small hill are buildings of massive stone slabs and lines of statue-menhirs which combine to give one an extraordinary sense of prehistoric life. The buildings which cover the site, the west, central and east monuments, are not easy for the layman to understand since they all became hybrids of two cultures, the later Torreen invaders obscuring the earlier megalithic settlement.

The sudden appearance, probably around 1400 BC, of menhirs carrying swords and daggers suggests an invasion. The early megalithic peoples of Filitosa were a pastoral society living in the Stone Age, unable to make metal weapons. Roger Grosjean suggested that the Torreens, a warlike people from the eastern Mediterranean, invaded southern Corsica and slowly drove the megalithic people further north where scattered remains have been found. Grosjean also believed that following traditions elsewhere, the statue-menhirs with weapons were Torreen victims killed in battle, made by the megalithic people who by this time had also learned from their invaders to work metal and make swords and daggers. The Torreens are named after the tower-like structures they favoured but their exact identity remains a mystery. It has been suggested that they were descendants of the Shardanes, a piratical seafaring people who had terrorised the Egyptians and other Mediterranean people as early as the second millennium. There is no doubt that in a final battle they overcame Filitosa and superimposed their own fortified buildings on the earlier megalithic settlement. Roughly speaking, the general form of Filitosa and the twenty or so menhirs represent the period of the peaceful, pastoral megalithic people. The impressive, superimposed stone structures are the later work of the Torreens who probably left Corsica for Sardinia around 800 BC.

I must emphasise that all I have written about Filitosa and the background of the megalithic culture and the Torreen invasion is the merest sketch of a variety of scholarly opinions which in their own turn are based largely on informed speculation. Every schoolboy knows that Stonehenge is surrounded by enigmas. It is the same with Filitosa and the uncertainty adds to the compelling mystery of the place.

Filitosa is a little off the beaten track but worth every effort to get there. Near the entrance is an excellent site museum which gives a clear account of the ruins in an attractive display. On the site re-erected menhirs stand like sentinels, around the central structure and in the valley below. That late afternoon in October the interplay of light and long shadows added a sense of awe and among the rocks below the ancient citadel the ground was brightly pink with hundreds of wild cyclamen. It is a beautiful and moving place.

The first time I came to Sartène it was the most sombre town in Corsica. The inhabitants were as silent and granite-faced as their tightly shuttered houses. We found a restaurant, an austere room with little light, no finesse and no menu. We were served by a gaunt woman in black who, without comment, placed bread and bowls of soup on our table, together with a carafe of rough local wine. The soup was followed by a pungent stew and goats' cheese with a sharp flavour that cut one's tongue. When we had finished she put the bill in front of me, took the money, gave me change and retired to her kitchen. Not a word had been exchanged from start to finish. There was nothing rude in the woman's manner. Her silence was not aimed at us. It was simply the way of Sartène. It was rooted in centuries of introverted life, isolation, and secretiveness. It was the code of behaviour of this area which encompassed everything that was strangest in Corsican life, including the relentless vendetta and the often related banditry.

Sartène is a brighter place today, at least on the surface. As we climbed from the valley of the Rizzanèse river, the tall houses of the town rose from their rocky foundations piling up in layers against the sky. Despite its forbidding medieval appearance it is not as old as it appears. It was founded by the Genoese in the early sixteenth century to protect the region from the frequent incursions by pirates from North Africa. But the town's defences were not sufficient to stop the Bey of Algiers from occupying the town in 1583 and taking 400 of the townspeople into slavery. Sited on this steep hill it cannot have been an easy town to capture and the Barbary pirates must have been as intrepid as they were menacing.

Brutality and violence were to stain the history of this town until the vendetta and banditry petered out during the first half of the nineteenth century. Yet even today, an atmosphere lingers on as disturbing as a cobweb across one's face. In the backstreet cafés the local men sit close around the tables linked in muttered conversation. Up and down the steep cobbled streets, the women sit silent before their inhospitable doors, guardians of their closed and secret family life. Tourists may chatter like noisy birds of passage over their rum cocktails and 'Knickerbocker Glories' in the bright sun of the main square. The real Sartène lives on in the claustrophobic shadows of the old alleys where honour rather than money is still the local currency. Linger here for a couple of days. You can see the few sights in two hours but you need time to attune your ear to the music of this strange place where even the stones of the old houses seem to cry out for vengeance. To understand Sartène you must learn all the nuances of a Corsican silence, deep and dark as an old well.

One event above all others exposes the soul of Sartène and that is the macabre Good Friday procession called *Le Catenacciu*, in which the agony of Christ's Passion has, over the centuries, been married to the obsessive emotions of the vendetta. Just inside the main door of the church of Ste-Marie, which dominates the main square, you can see the penitential wooden cross and chain of the procession. The oak cross weighs 31.5 kg, the chain – from which the procession derives its name – weighs 14 kg. *Le Catenacciu*, the penitent, follows in the footsteps of Christ for three hours along his own road to Golgotha dragging a burden of over 45 kg. I have often shuddered at that strange blend of Christianity, sadism and masochism that marks southern Mediterranean devotions. I shuddered again at the cross and chains of Sartène and wondered if sins of violence are really expiated by this imitation of Christ's suffering.

Holy Week has produced strange rites in many places but the procession of Sartène is among the strangest. A French guidebook compares it with the Holy Week processions in Seville, Spain. It is a false comparison. During Seville's *Semana Santa*, despite the throbbing drums and the hooded penitents, it is a festival that throughout the week looks forward to the hope of the Resurrection. It lasts for several nights and as the glittering floats stagger by, the spectators in the cafés put down their glasses and rise unsteadily from their seats to cross themselves. A hooded penitent nudges the youth next to him, hands over his tall candle, and gathering up his robes races for the nearest public lavatory. It is a solemn pageant but it is saved from being sinister by remaining a pageant of life, being 'caught short' an unselfconscious saving grace.

There is not a touch of humour to lighten the sombre procession of Sartène. It is a re-enactment of the walk to Golgotha with strange Corsican overtones. The parish priest chooses the chief penitent and his identity is a solemn secret. It is said that many apply for this opportunity to obtain forgiveness for the gravest sins; in the past, criminals, bandits and murderers. *Le Catenacciu* spends the previous night in prayer concealed in a neighbouring convent. In the procession he appears in a robe and pointed hood of red, the chain dragging from one ankle of his bare feet, the cross on his shoulder. He is accompanied by a second anonymous penitent clad in white, who represents Simon of Cyrene. They are followed by a procession of other penitents in black robes and hoods carrying a wooden figure of Christ together with the local clergy. The procession winds through the town accompanied by traditional Corsican songs. Three times the chief penitent falls as Christ fell and with each painful step he is freed from his oppressive sin.

In the central Place de la Libération two large cafés occupy the west side. The last of the tourists and a few more prosperous locals lounged in wicker chairs gazing over their rum punches at the Arab workers who smoked endlessly on the hard benches opposite. On the eastern side, the square opens onto a terrace which commands a view of the valley spreading away far below. To the left of the church is the former palace of the Genoese governor, today the Hôtel de Ville. It is a small yet massive building and an archway through the middle leads to the old town, the quarter of Santa Anna, a maze of narrow lanes and alleyways shut in by tall stone houses topheavy with iron balconies, festoons of washing and drunken chimney pots. The houses and the old fortifications are all one and flights of steps lead up and down the hillside, in a few places the houses joined by overhead bridges. In places the alleys are hardly more than slits between the walls, the black shadow ending in a sudden bright slice of distant landscape.

The owner of our hotel was a pleasant antidote to the oppressive atmosphere of this brooding town. She was Vietnamese and many years before had married a Corsican. She had that neat but plump charm of many middle-aged oriental women. 'My husband is a devout Catholic but I am a Buddhist. I will never change.' The difference of opinion seemed to have provided a sure footing for a long and happy marriage. She took us into her office where the walls and cabinets were covered with pictures and statues of esoteric images of the Buddha. It was touching to see how much they meant to her, a few garish posters and tawdry statues binding her to her distant past. The exotic, happy iconography seemed all the more unusual in this town of dark faith.

We made our first excursion from Sartène to the north-east, an area which offers violent history and beautiful countryside in about equal measure. Dropping down into the valley of the Rizzanèse river, we came to the most picturesque Genoese bridge in Corsica, the Spin' A Cavallu. The stone bridge and its setting are so perfect that it had remained in my memory over a quarter of a century more vividly than anything else in Corsica. The place is as lovely as ever but in twenty-five years the surrounding trees have grown obscuring the main buttresses of the bridge on either bank. Now the hump-backed span of stone seems to fly from the thicket on either bank but its elegant reflection is still caught in the trembling water of the river which moves gently over a bed of rock and stones. The Genoese built many bridges in Corsica but this is said to be the best-preserved, first built during the thirteenth century. From the river bank, despite its heavy stonework, the bridge looks light and narrow. Crossing it one can see its substantial construction with width enough for two horses.

We drove on to the mountain village of Fozzano, the setting of one of Corsica's most celebrated vendettas, partly because of its own prolonged violence and partly because it inspired Prosper Mérimée's famous novel of the vendetta, *Colomba*. Today, Fozzano is a quiet and attractive village but the *scenery* of the vendetta remains. There had been a deep political division in the village since the eighteenth century splitting the community into two factions led by the Durazzo and the Carabelli families. This bitter antagonism flared up outside the church after mass on the feast of the Holy Trinity in 1830. Insults were exchanged, swords and knives flashed and three men died, a Durazzo and two men of the Carabelli faction. One year later there was a second encounter in the maquis and another Carabelli died. Colomba Bartoli, a widow in her fifties, is reputed to have been the most implacable leader of the Carabelli faction and she now demanded vengeance. In 1833 an ambush was arranged and two men of each faction were killed, one of them Colomba's son. Peace was made finally the following year at a ceremony in the church at Sartène but a terrible bitterness darkened the life of the village for many more years.

Mérimée came to Fozzano in 1839 and met the formidable Colomba Bartoli who was then sixty-four. The meeting inspired his novel but although he borrowed her name and captured faithfully the spirit of the Corsican vendetta he changed the setting and the character of his own heroine. It remains the best novel about the Corsican vendetta but Mérimée did not face up to the wholly unromantic brutality and ugliness of his subject. Had he done so he could have used Colomba Bartoli for his central character rather than softening his theme by the introduction of a beautiful heroine.

If you have read *Colomba* and are familiar with the dark realities of the vendetta, so numerous in this region, you may find Fozzano a confusing place. The village now spreads peacefully down the hillside, neat and tidy with geraniums cascading from the balconies of attractive houses. Even the inhabitants seem keen to obliterate memories of the past. I was walking round the upper town looking for the Durazzo house when a man asked if he could help me. I said that I was looking for the buildings associated with the Colomba vendetta. He gave me a regretful look and retired into his house.

The buildings are still there. Near the centre of the town are the towering, fortified houses of the rival families, as stark as the enmity which made them necessary. Below Colomba's house, on the edge of the village, is a small and dilapidated chapel, containing the tomb of her son. This rugged and decaying little piece of architecture is a poignant monument to the blind hatred that must have made life in this isolated village insufferable for over a hundred years. Despite the sunshine and the bright flowers Fozzano still has echoes of the vendetta.

Nearby is the village of Santa Maria-Figaniella, worth visiting for its small but elegant Pisan church, built in the twelfth century and still used as the parish church. Its architectural grace has been unbalanced by the erection of a heavy and much later belltower, freestanding but elbowing the small Pisan apse. The church is enclosed by a wall which you must climb if you wish to examine the decoration. The mellow but plain stonework is relieved by an arcaded frieze which runs round the walls below the roof. The small consoles supporting the arches are carved with geometrical designs and with animals and grotesque heads. The sculpture has a genuine quality but the real wonder is that the Pisan masons bothered at all in such obscure settlements. The perfect simplicity of the architecture, the precision of the masonry and the restrained ornament produce an austere beauty which is part of the romanesque genius.

In the mountains to the east is the village of Carbini, a ragged place but with a fine church and an ancient history dark and sinister even by the standards of this sombre region. It was here that a group of people, following heretical beliefs, established a mystical, collective society drawing inspiration from an ideal of primitive Christianity. They were called the *Giovannali* after the local church of San Giovanni where they held some of their meetings. Rumour soon went out that these meetings were in fact orgies of adultery and sodomy. When the heresy spread over the south of Corsica the Pope excommunicated them and foreign troops and Corsicans hunted them down and destroyed them.

It seems certain that the rumours of orgies and sexual rites were no more than the usual propaganda put out to suppress new religions. The *Giovannali* had respectable roots in the lay Third Order of St Francis which was widespread in Corsica, encouraged by the Franciscan friars of the island. At this time there was a great schism in the Franciscan order itself. Many friars felt that the order had moved away from the austere way of life ordained by the founder. Communities broke away to follow the primitive rule of St Francis. Amongst the Third Order, both in Corsica and mainland France, this led certain groups to practise the 'evangelical poverty' preached by Christ. Such beliefs flowered in Carbini and elsewhere as a kind of spiritual communism in which everything was held in common. Such dangerous and subversive thinking could not be tolerated by local bishops or by the Pope and the heretics were stamped out by the combined forces of papal troops and the Inquisition. Even today that ruthless act of destruction lingers like a shadow over the mean hovels of Carbini.

A final excursion to the south of Sartène takes one to two interesting megalithic sites and a brighter landscape. For some reason these early Corsicans always seemed to build their settlements in pleasant, rural surroundings which leave their remains in a pleasing arcadian setting. It was probably because the hinterland between the mountains and the sea provided an environment suitable for their way of life. Driving first to the Mégalithes de Cauria, you turn left off the main road and follow a well-signposted track to the official car park. We left our car here with true British obedience and walked through two kilometres of vineyards and maquis to the site. When we arrived there we found that French and German picnickers had brought their cars along the footpath. You can take your choice.

It is a wide, rolling landscape here, a thorny maquis surrounding fields, small thickets and rocky hillocks. A line of worn menhirs stand by the entrance. If they ever had features they have long vanished. It is more likely that the shaped pillars were made before the sculpture broke into a primitive portraiture. Along a path and over a couple of typically badly made Corsican stiles is the Dolmen of Fontanaccia, the largest and best-preserved dolmen in Corsica. On six vertical slabs of granite 1.60 m high the megalithic builders placed a massive slab roof to form some kind of burial chamber. The building stands on a raised piece of ground, impressive and intriguing, leaving one wondering how these enormous stones can have been manhandled to form this precarious structure. The inspiration must have come from the surrounding hillocks where nature had already created great formations of granite slabs and boulders which in places appear like designed buildings. But how primitive men imitated nature remains a mystery.

When reading about megalithic culture I had been intrigued by the strange way megalithic architecture had spread around the world, far beyond the bounds of Europe. There is no discernible pattern of dissemination or common chronology but the remains everywhere share common features. One authority claimed that megalithic remains existed in Japan. This surprised me since I know Japan well and had never come across anything remotely megalithic in this culture of wooden buildings.

In the spring of 1987, just after I had finished the first draft of this book, I returned to my home in Japan for three months. In June I drove around southern Japan researching another book and returned to Kyoto via Asuka, the cradle of Japanese civilisation which I had not visited before. There I found the famous seventh-century tomb called *Ishibutai*. The central tomb chamber, originally covered by extensive earthworks but now exposed, was in effect a Japanese dolmen. It is much larger than Fontanaccia and the lower part of the chamber is sunk into the ground but the basic design and construction of balanced, massive slabs of stone is in the same architectural tradition as the Corsican tomb. There are other tomb chambers of this type in Japan but *Ishibutai* is the largest.

Further along the path is another large group of menhirs, forty of different heights ranged in two ranks beneath the trees. This is called the Alignement de Renaggiu. Apart from the great dolmen there are no remains of other buildings on this site or any signs of what must have been a considerable settlement. But in its quiet isolation it is an impressive place with the same strange atmosphere of Filitosa. I enjoyed it all, including rescuing an extremely stout German lady from the top of a collapsing stile.

If you return to the main road and continue south, after a short distance you will see the second megalithic site of the area signposted on the right. A short dirt road brings you to Palaggiu, the largest collection of menhirs in Corsica. A hundred stone figures stand or lie toppled in the seeming disarray of a battlefield. The site is interesting for the quantity if not the quality though if you examine the menhirs closely you will find some traces of engraving representing swords and the Torreen influence. Faced with so many menhir-figures it is easy to forget the achievement they represent and the effort that must have gone into the shaping of each one of these early monuments. I thought this area fascinating and complementary to the more famous Filitosa. Taken all together the megalithic sites seem symbolically to present the granite roots of Corsican history, the Torreens precursors of all the barbaric invaders to besiege the island in the future.

6

The Imperial City
AJACCIO

Napoleon Bonaparte was born in Ajaccio on 15 August 1769. Later, in honour of this event, the town was named the 'Imperial City' but neither titles nor marble statues can give a small, provincial seaside town a convincing aura of imperial splendour. 'On a wet day,' grumbled Edward Lear in 1868, 'it would be hard to find so dull a place as Ajaccio.' His view of the inhabitants was no more flattering. 'Says a Frenchman to me, and truly – speaking of the slow-walking people in the Piazza here – "these Corsicans walk like cripples or snails." '

There were other British who, as early as the 1860s, found Ajaccio attractive enough to settle there. They built themselves 'cottages' around the new Anglican church and the colony remained popular until the Second World War. This British outpost was pioneered by a Scottish spinster, Thomasina Campbell, described by Lear as 'a vast and man-like maiden who roars and raves about Corsica'. The description has the poetic lilt of one of his limericks. Miss Campbell was one of that indomitable breed of British women who swept round the world during the nineteenth century brushing off danger like houseflies. She built herself a substantial villa with a touch of Gothic decoration and was the leader in the building of the Anglican church. She travelled all over Corsica, indifferent to the threat of bandits or malaria and published her travels in *Southward Ho!*, an unromantic account of the island reflecting the author's down-to-earth approach to life. Edward Lear was to find her helpful during his stay in Ajaccio. 'The kindly Miss C.' gave him practical advice, a travelling flask and a stern warning against the coachman he had hired. Not far from Ajaccio the man drove the coach over a cliff but luckily Lear and his servant were walking at that moment.

Ajaccio is set in a magnificent position on the north shore of a great bay which stretches 17 km from the Iles Sanguinaires to the southern promontory, the Punta Guardiola. Even Lear had a good word for this panoramic view. When I first came to Ajaccio twenty-five years ago, it was still the quiet town that had attracted those nineteenth-century expatriates, set in the unspoilt surroundings of the mountains and the maquis. Today, the town has more vitality and sophistication but prosperity is eroding its charm, destroying the balance between the town and its natural surroundings with highrise flats and industrial development.

There are memories from the past but they become harder to recapture. We were sitting in the worn rattan chairs of a pavement café which retained an old-fashioned air. The waiters fostered the illusion. In white shirts and black waistcoats they pirouetted between the marble-topped tables, balancing trays of *pastis* and *citron pressé* and sweating in the hot October sun. But at our feet, hardly a metre away, unending lines of cars surged by, snarling and hooting their way up and down the Cours Napoléon. Cars have taken over Ajaccio, polluting its narrow streets with frenzy, noise and fumes. Who wants to sit in a café when it becomes difficult to tell if you are sipping lemonade or gasoline? There is plenty of interest to see in Ajaccio but it is not the attractive town it used to be.

This is Napoleon's town but when one looks at his early life it is easy to see why he retained little affection for his birthplace. On his way back from Egypt in 1799 he spent one week in Ajaccio but after that he never visited Corsica again. And throughout his reign he made only the most meagre provision for the island, a parsimony which was continued by the French authorities until recently. Ajaccio is now full of Napoleonic monuments. None was provided by Napoleon.

In 1769 Napoleon's parents, Carlo and Letizia Bonaparte, were living in Corte where Carlo, a shiftless lawyer, was working as secretary to the liberal leader, Pasquale Paoli. At that moment the Genoese sold out to the French whose troops swarmed over the island. Paoli fled to England and the Bonapartes, Letizia already pregnant, fled over the mountains on mules to Ajaccio, a rugged prenatal journey which perhaps had some influence on Napoleon's character. The family settled in the substantial house now on show as Napoleon's birthplace though at that time they could afford to occupy only the first floor. There is a story that Letizia felt the child arriving while she was attending mass in a local church. By the time she reached home she was too weak to get upstairs and Napoleon was born on the ground floor. The birthplace has now become so much of a museum that its layout bears little relation to the early occupation by the family.

I find the birthplace lacking any authentic atmosphere. It hovers between being a house and a museum and the dingy provincial grandeur of the present furnishings belong to a later period. After Napoleon's success in the Italian campaign the family were able to take over the whole house and to decorate and furnish it in a grander style. But this was not the home that Napoleon knew as a child. He must have grown up in a more threadbare world, penury never far from the family's elbow. By the time of the aggrandisement of the family home, Carlo was dead, Letizia stayed only a year or two before leaving for Paris and Napoleon saw it briefly during his visit of 1799. After that no member of the family ever lived there again. Perhaps this explains why the atmosphere of a museum obscures any sense of a house and a home. The neat rows of Empire chairs and the faded locks of hair in gilt frames do not succeed in bringing Napoleon to life or creating an atmosphere worthy of the momentous occasion of his birth.

The house faces a narrow street which widens slightly to form a mean little square. The high houses and the tight alleys between them make the whole area claustrophobic. Whatever the mule ride may have contributed, it was here that the character of Napoleon was formed and it was in the rough and tumble of these streets that he earned himself the nickname of 'the troublemaker'. His father set about buttressing the family fortunes by ingratiating himself with the French authorities, in particular the Comte de Marbeuf, the military governor. Carlo played up a distant connection with noble Florentine ancestors and, having established his rank with Marbeuf, succeeded in obtaining a scholarship for Napoleon at the military academy at Brienne and the *Ecole Militaire* in Paris, together with educational privileges for his other children. The position of the family seemed to be improving though the official recognition and posts enjoyed by Carlo brought more honour than income. In 1779, at the age of nine, Napoleon left the island to begin his military training at Brienne, going on to the school in Paris in 1784 and emerging as a lieutenant of the artillery when he was sixteen. At this stage he remained a Corsican patriot with only modest ambitions for his future.

The French Revolution led to the return of Paoli from exile in England. He soon fell out with the French revolutionary government and again declared Corsica independent. This left the Bonaparte family on the wrong side. Their house in Ajaccio was attacked and looted while Letizia and her younger children hid in the maquis. The family were rescued by Napoleon but were forced to flee in penury to Toulon. Paoli's second republic did not last long and by 1795 he was again on his way to England. By 1796 the French had regained control over Corsica.

Carlo Bonaparte had died in Montpellier in 1785 but Letizia returned to live in Ajaccio for a few years before removing to Paris. The Bonapartes had not enjoyed an easy life in Corsica and the final indignity of their enforced flight to Toulon hardened memory into lasting bitterness. During his final days in exile on St Helena Napoleon was overtaken by a nostalgia for his birthplace, scenting the maquis in his memory and leaving instructions that he should be buried in Ajaccio if he was not allowed to be buried in Paris. He was buried in Paris and the martial splendour of Les Invalides underlines the meanness of the Napoleonic monuments in the town of his birth. Ajaccio was never adorned with the ornaments of an imperial city. Napoleon never forgave his compatriots for the humility and disgrace that they inflicted on his family and his own reputation. The few monuments in Ajaccio were erected after the Emperor's death and not at his command.

Indirectly, Napoleon was responsible for Ajaccio being endowed with the magnificent collection of paintings at the Fesch Museum. Joseph Fesch, a step-uncle of Napoleon, was a priest in

Ajaccio with a passion for painting and, for his time, an unusual breadth of taste. Napoleon appointed his uncle Archbishop of Lyons and he became Cardinal and Minister-Plenipotentiary to the Holy See. Seldom can such a blatant piece of nepotism have had such splendid results. The ambition of Cardinal Fesch was simple, his opportunities almost unlimited. He wished to form a collection of paintings which would illustrate the whole history of European art with outstanding works by all the great masters. The wars and revolutions that shook Europe at this time made available in one way or another masterpieces of every kind. By his death in 1839, the Cardinal had gone a long way in creating an encyclopedic collection, said to number some 30,000 paintings. He himself had lost count.

After Napoleon's death the Cardinal had fallen from favour and had been deprived of his archbishopric. He let it be known that if he were officially reinstated, he would bequeath his whole collection of paintings to the city of Lyons. When his offer was ignored he devised a new scheme whereby he would endow and build an academy in Ajaccio for which he would select a representative collection of one thousand paintings, a quality microcosm of the larger display of European paintings. The academy was built but the Cardinal died before he had made the selection of paintings for Ajaccio. The residuary legatee, Joseph Bonaparte, contested the will and by a compromise settlement was allowed to choose the pictures to be given to Ajaccio. Ironically, he snatched greedily at all the later painters then in fashion and sent off to Ajaccio a collection of Italian primitives which only the wide and farsighted taste of the Cardinal had appreciated.

With this attempt to fob off Ajaccio with the dross of the collection, the Fesch Museum in Ajaccio now owns the finest collection of early Italian painting in France outside the Louvre. There are important primitive paintings of the fourteenth century and works by many of the Italian masters of the fifteenth and sixteenth centuries: Botticelli, Cosimo Tura, Titian and Veronese. The museum is the most rewarding attraction in Ajaccio but I must warn readers that when I was there in October 1986, the museum was closed for a complete and long-needed

9 Morosaglia, birthplace of Pasquale Paoli, La Castagniccia

10 View through the chestnut forests, La Castagniccia

11 View across Roman ruins to Genoese fortress, Aleria

12 Stairway leading to the Roman Praetoria, Aleria

renovation. I asked at the Ajaccio tourist office when the museum would reopen. They were pessimistic. Lack of money has slowed down the work and they thought it unlikely that the museum would open again for at least two years and possibly three. If you are going to Corsica in the hope of seeing the Fesch Museum, you would be wise to find out first from the French Government Tourist Office if the museum is open again. I have exciting memories of seeing the collection many years ago but I hope that during this long closure the opportunity is being taken to clean the more important paintings.

Further along the Rue Cardinal Fesch stands the Chapelle impériale, built at the order of Napoleon III between 1857 and 1859, following a wish expressed in Cardinal Fesch's will. The chapel was designed in the Renaissance style by the crown architect, Paccard, and was consecrated in 1860. Then, the remains of Letizia and her half-brother, the Cardinal, having been brought from a cemetery in Italy, were interred in the new crypt. Napoleon's father, Carlo, lies near his wife and the other four tombs are occupied by noticeably minor members of the imperial family. The main church, with monochrome painted decorations by a local architect, Jérôme Maglioli, is well kept but oppressively unused. The imperial crypt, its arcaded tombs and central altar dressed in local marble, has a quiet solemnity but little sense of imperial grandeur. One cannot escape the feeling that one is watching a stage without the leading actor and with inadequate scenery for such a play. Napoleon Bonaparte lies buried in Paris and one cannot ignore his absence.

Across the road from the imperial mausoleum is the small confraternity chapel of St-Roch. The interior is well worn, the darkness broken only by the shaft of light in the doorway and a rack of candles burning before the quaint statue of the patron saint. People of the neighbourhood come and go, kneeling with moving lips before the saint. Doubtless, he promises salvation, to find your lost spectacles or to help your daughter through her school exam. It is the kind of shabby, used church that restores your faith, if not in God, at least in the sanctity of human nature.

The Rue Cardinal Fesch twists and narrows sothwards

towards the cramped quarters of the old town. Attractive shops offer Corsican foods and wine and up the side alleys the housefronts lean intimately towards one another. It should have the character of a secret world but most of the time it explodes into a confusion of impatient traffic, frenzied drivers fighting their way through the barricades of parked vans. It is a relief to break out of this noisome claustrophobia into the shaded, quieter space of the rectangular Place Maréchal-Foch. At the west end of the square, set amongst tall palms, neat hedges and beds of bright begonias stands the Fountain of the Four Lions. Four gruff-looking beasts crouch on their bronze haunches spewing water from their mouths and guarding the high pedestal on which Napoleon stands, disguised in white marble as the First Consul. The toga fits well enough but the expression is vacuous. It is difficult to take this classical charade too seriously but the statue adds a certain provincial grandeur to the coolness and comparative quietness of the square. The marble benches are shared by the older inhabitants and Arab émigrés. Both eye the tourist with an abject disapproval.

Apart from the statue, the Place leads from its south-west end to Napoleon's birthplace and on its north side to another collection of imperial relics. The Hôtel de Ville has a plain classical façade and a more ornamental clocktower. The first floor houses the Musée Napoléonien whose memorabilia range from a photocopy of Napoleon's birth certificate to a lean-faced death mask taken in St Helena. The main room of the museum is like a large and overfurnished salon. Of all the busts and portraits that crowd around the walls, none is more lacking in real vitality than the painting by Gérard of Napoleon in his coronation robes.

The custodian in charge of this collection was a lady of both energy and enterprise. Plump beyond the limits of her cotton dress, her hair dyed a colour reminiscent of tabby cats, she swept towards us like a great hostess and told us that in five minutes she would be giving a conducted tour of the collection. We had been warned. A glance around the cluttered walls had already convinced me that three minutes on my own would be enough but Madame must have read my thoughts. Just as I was retreating from the Gérard to the door, Madame appeared with a large key and locked it. Her tour was long and boring. She was wise to assure herself a captive audience.

There was a further fiasco with the two young women in the Ajaccio tourist office next door to the Hôtel de Ville. The French National Tourist Office in London had kindly written to the tourist authorities in Ajaccio asking them to give me any help I might need. I did not really want any help but thought it polite to call and to say that I was enjoying my tour of Corsica. Not to my surprise, the tourist office had never heard of me. The girls were pleasant but not disposed to make great efforts on my behalf. One did find the energy to get up and in a perfunctory way to riffle through a file of letters. But no, nothing had been received from London. Looking back, I now think that I was in the wrong place; the local tourist office rather than the National Tourist Office but these lethargic girls may not have been aware of the other place. They did persuade me to *buy* their official map of Ajaccio. It looked amateur and when I examined it closely I found that by a printing error, the map references placed all the major sightseeing attractions of Ajaccio in deep water a kilometre to the east of the port. I have often pondered on a suitable English translation for that familiar French tourist institution, the Syndicat d'Initiative. Now I think I know.

To the south of the Place Maréchal Foch lies the heart of the old town enclosed on the east side by the Genoese citadel and the old port. The heavy walls of the citadel slope down into a deep, dry moat but it is a functional piece of fortification without the romantic outlines of the citadels at Bonifacio, Calvi and Bastia. One is not allowed to enter since the fortress is now used by the army. The narrow streets forming the old town to the west of the citadel are again Genoese in character. The tall, peeling houses topple towards each other, keeping the streets sunless and gloomy. The streets near Napoleon's birthplace are busy with cafés and souvenir shops but further away commerce and every sign of life have departed leaving the area shuttered and silent.

Opposite the entrance to the citadel where a young sentry stands on duty you will find a small and different kind of museum.

The Musée du Capitellu is privately owned and has an interesting collection of the possessions of an old Ajaccian family which evokes the life of the town in the eighteenth and nineteenth centuries. Around the corner is the church of St-Érasme, built by the Jesuits in 1617, closed at the time of the French Revolution and in 1815 opened again in the name of the saint who is patron of sailors and fishermen. Inside, there are offertory models of boats, a collection of fine vestments including a chasuble which belonged to Cardinal Fesch and three striking figures of the crucified Christ mounted on processional crosses.

Further along the street, facing a small square, stands the cathedral of Ajaccio, built in the Renaissance style on the site of the older church of Ste-Croix. Building started in 1582 to the grandiose plans of Pope Gregory XIII's architect, Giacomo della Porta, but a lack of funds resulted in a smaller building finished in 1593. A plaque by the main door expresses regret that it was not possible to build the larger church. Today, a general dustiness and dilapidation in the interior suggests a continuing lack of funds and I was particularly disappointed to find that the main attraction of the cathedral, a painting of the Virgin by Eugène Delacroix, had been removed from its altar. There was no explanation; only a richly framed rectangle of Renaissance brickwork.

Otherwise, with its clutter of devotional bric-à-brac, it was a pleasing church. The elaborate marble altars reached a crescendo of solemn splendour in the high altar presented by Napoleon's younger sister, Elisa Bacciochi, in 1811, while a medley of saints peered down from their niches through the devotional gloom broken here and there by trembling patches of candlelight.

Napoleon had been here, at an early age. To the right of the main door is the white marble font where the future Emperor of France was baptised on 21 July 1771, approaching his second birthday. It was a surprising delay for a devout Corsican family and, possibly, a difficult age at which to enrol a lusty child into the Christian family. In 1900 an elaborate bronze cover in the Renaissance style was added to the font. I thought it looked more like a miniature and bizarre spire off a Gaudi church but it certainly makes the font more conspicuous. On the first pillar to the left of the entrance is a tablet engraved with Napoleon's last instruction from St Helena:

> Si on proscrit de Paris mon cadavre comme on a proscrit ma personne, je souhaite qu'on m'inhume auprès de mes ancêtres dans la cathédrale d'Ajaccio, en Corse.

Ajaccio might seem a more genuine place of Napoleonic pilgrimage if this last wish had come true. But the honour fell to Paris and not even in death was the old bitterness healed. Indeed, there is a kind of bitter irony in making his birthplace his second choice.

Down by the port where the cars cannot follow, there is a brighter holiday mood with multi-coloured boats bobbing on their moorings along the marina, enticing restaurants shaded by planes and palms near the quay and glorious views out over the Gulf of Ajaccio. Here, away from the frenzy of the town centre, one can still enjoy the lazy atmosphere of an older Ajaccio. But if you look over the houses that line the quay, you will find the surrounding hills and mountains already half-hidden behind the rising lines of geometrical apartment blocks, a growing urban monotony. I lowered my eyes again and walked out along the Jetée de la Citadelle where there are excellent facilities for the small boats visiting Ajaccio. I enjoyed looking down at these boats, their occupants eating gargantuan alfresco lunches squeezed around tables on the poop-deck. Nearby, an elderly Englishman clambered over the wheelhouse of an old Cornish fishing boat while he gave fatherly advice to a young American who had just arrived in a million-dollar cruiser. Between eating and carrying out running repairs, I couldn't help wondering if these amateur sailors would inspect the historic sights of Ajaccio or, for that matter, any of the other places they visited.

When we first arrived in Ajaccio we had searched the centre of the town for a hotel in a quiet situation. It was hopeless and we decided to try a hotel recommended in one of our guide-books to the north of the town. The hotel did not look much and it was a dingy area. But at least the hotel was up a quiet side street, out of earshot of the stream of traffic on the main coast road. Inside, the hotel was comfortable, the staff pleasant and with a room at the back we enjoyed three quiet nights. To one side of the hotel's car park was a pleasant, simple restaurant, noteworthy for its single waitress. She was a large, tousled blonde, a heroine straight out of *Tom Jones*, her ample bosom all but spilling out of her blouse. When we arrived for dinner the large restaurant was empty and this statuesque, rural goddess welcomed us with a warming smile that never left her lips, or her eyes, the entire evening. We chatted as she took our order and recommended the house wine. Yes, her husband did the cooking and she managed the dining room alone. At that moment it seemed no problem.

Five minutes later two busloads of German tourists surged through the door and filled every table. Our bucolic waitress was unperturbed. She swept around the tables with the furious energy of a dancing dervish; collecting orders, patiently explaining the menu, sorting out the wine list and, after brief consultations at the kitchen hatch, serving food and wine without pause or error. Ninety minutes later everyone was fed, all five courses of the set menu. It was a delightful kind of miracle and that ebullient woman was still smiling, with just a drop or two of perspiration trickling from her soft, disordered hair. Her effort was the most Napoleonic thing I saw in all Ajaccio.

Before we left Ajaccio, we felt that we ought to drive out to the northern end of the bay to get a closer view of the Iles Sanguinaires. The coast road leaves the centre of the town to run below a new suburb of expensive apartment complexes which climb up the mountainside. Here and there were older, grand villas with well-kept gardens and a few luxurious hotels. One of these was heavily defended by the police. Apart from one or two snipers half-concealed in the shrubbery of neighbouring gardens high above the road, the area immediately around the hotel was patrolled by gendarmes on foot, speed cops on ferocious white motorcycles and, in reserve, two armoured buses packed with a small army of *les flics*. I have no idea what they were all doing there. Perhaps a possible target for the *séparatistes* was staying in the hotel. To be fair, it was one of the few occasions when I saw a policeman in Corsica. The military presence in the island was more evident.

This was the only excitement of our excursion. The Punta de la Parata did offer a magnificent view across the Bay of Ajaccio and had we been there for the recommended sunset, we might have found everything more breathtaking. Instead, it was a grey and chilly afternoon and the single café, flanked by concrete terraces and tables of shivering tourists, was as disheartening as the litter which decorated the car park below. The sunset would have been beautiful and the falling darkness would have shrouded the dreariness of the viewing point. There is much to be said for obeying the instructions of one's guide-book. A spirit of independence can lead one into some disappointing situations. My own final advice would be to visit Ajaccio – but not for too long.

7

The Corsican Capital
CORTE

The small town of Corte does no justice to its epic place in Corsican history. As you drive over the Pont Tavignano, the silhouette of the citadel rises on a truncated stump of rock, diminished by the line of mountains behind. The old town sprawls up the eastern slope; white walls pierced by lines of square windows and capped by low orange roofs. The opposite side is more precipitous, a tumbling wall of rough rock softened near its base where it plunges into a cluster of slender trees along the river. The top of the citadel is surrounded by plain, heavy fortifications which enclose only a forlorn group of seeming domestic buildings. This first view of Corte does have a certain homespun charm but it is not the setting one had expected for Corsica's own capital and the scene of so much heroic history.

Corte lies at the heart of Corsica, geographically and historically. Although it was only the official capital of independent Corsica from 1755 to 1769, for centuries the town had been the symbol and the rallying point for Corsican independence. The insurgence of the eighteenth century and Pasquale Paoli's bid for freedom was only the last of many attempts by the Corsicans to free themselves from foreign domination. Paoli made Corte his official capital but long before that the town had been a battleground in various struggles for independence. It is said that in the ninth century Corsican patriots drove the occupying Saracens from Corte. It is possible that the ninth-century pre-Pisan church and baptistery of St-Jean, whose ruins stand 3 km to the south of the town, were first built as a celebration of this victory over the infidel. At the same moment Corte became the symbol of a free Corsica.

Corte was always a small and architecturally undistinguished town, its sleepy streets and mean houses huddling close on the lower slopes of the citadel. The Corsicans never had a taste or the money for much ceremony. For them, a tool that did the job, however rough-hewn, was a good tool. Corte stands at the centre of the island, in the heart of Corsica's mountains. It is the gateway between the north and the south or, in older terms, between the Diqua and the Dila dai Monti. Today good or reasonable roads run from Corte north and south and to the east and west coasts, passing gently through river valleys or, more precariously, through the mountain gorges that stretch away to the west of Corte. In earlier days some of these journeys could be made only along the shepherds' tracks that hung along the steep mountainsides but they were well known and well trodden by shepherds and insurgents alike. It was this central position, isolated from the foreign-occupied coastal towns by the ramparts of the surrounding mountains, that made Corte the centre for Corsican nationalism and its frequent struggles for independence.

From the fourteenth to the sixteenth century Corte suffered from its key position in the island's communications. The Genoese took possession of Corte when they settled in Corsica and held it until the early fifteenth century. The powerful, treacherous seigneurial families of the south ruled their lands in independence and had they possessed the mutual trust to unite, they might have driven the Genoese out of Corsica and established an independent kingdom. They preferred to make trouble by siding with Genoa's enemies, the Pisans and the Kingdom of Aragon, who both had dreams of a Mediterranean empire. One of the Cinarchesi warlords, the brave but ruthless Vincentello d'Istria, sided with Aragon and in 1419 drove the Genoese out of Corte and the following year built the citadel. He received little help in his campaign from the Spanish but following his success against the Genoese he was appointed Viceroy of Corsica. Even after the Spanish withdrawal, following their failure to capture Bonifacio in 1420, Vincentello continued to rule a large part of the island for another fourteen years.

Vincentello had inherited the military and political skills of his Cinarchesi ancestors and a portion of their bad blood. Sinucello della Rocca had also, in the thirteenth century, nearly established an independent Corsican kingdom but, old and blinded by venereal disease, he was handed over to the Genoese by his bastard son. Similar strains of greed and sensuality led to the overthrow of Vincentello. Despite a sinister appearance with malformed arms and a face disfigured by crinkled skin and a gross wart like an eye fallen from its socket, he was a great womaniser, achieving his way by will or force. But when he increased taxes and raped the betrothed daughter of a fellow nobleman his supporters turned against him and betrayed him to the Genoese. In 1434 he was executed in Genoa. It is hard to decide whether the history of the Cinarchesi would be best portrayed by grand opera or Grand Guignol.

Unrest, at times approaching anarchy, continued in Corsica. In 1453 the Genoese put the island under the protection of the Office of St George, a powerful organisation with its own army. It tightened control in Corsica, strengthening fortifications all over the island and taking possession of Corte. In turn the Office of St George suffered the last attack by the Cinarchesi led by Rinuccio della Rocca until the rebellion came to an end with his assassination in 1511. Apart from a brief respite, rebellion broke out again in 1533. It was sponsored by the strange alliance of Henry II of France who invaded Corsica with the help of a Turkish fleet. The French force was led by Sampiero Corso, born into a shepherd family in the village of Bastellica, and now a mercenary and a colonel in the French army but a Corsican patriot at heart.

Sampiero Corso is another legendary figure, a legend and Corsican hero in his own lifetime. When he was sent by his French commander to take possession of Corte, the people of the town came out and gave him the keys. Sampiero's early career mirrors that of a number of distinguished Corsicans who came after him, not least Napoleon. Leaving the island to become a mercenary in the service of the Medicis of Florence, eventually he made his reputation in the French army of Henry II fighting in the war against Charles V. At Perpignon he saved the life of the dauphin, was granted the right to a coat of arms which included the royal *fleur de lys d'or* and by 1547 was made commander of the

Corsican regiment of infantry. At the age of forty-nine he married the fifteen-year-old Vannina d'Ornano, daughter of one of the noblest families in Corsica. This led to tragedy. In 1563, Sampiero strangled his wife. The Ornano family may have been treasonably involved with the Genoese but there have been suggestions of jealousy and other motifs. When Flaubert visited Corsica as a young man he became interested in the story. Seeing it as a plot for a novel he wrote to an acquaintance in Ajaccio for more information. He received no answer, dropped the idea and, possibly, the great Corsican novel was lost.

Whatever Sampiero's motifs, he remained in favour with the French court but France gave up the Corsican campaign in 1559 when they returned the island to the Genoese, following the Treaty of Cateau-Cambrésis. But Sampiero did not give up his struggle for Corsican independence. In 1564 he landed with a small force in the Gulf of Valinco and he was soon supported by an army of Corsicans in this new rebellion against the Genoese. By 1567 Sampiero was in control of most of the island. But on his way home to Bastelica, through the treachery of the Ornano family, he was ambushed, his body hacked to pieces and his head raised on a pike by the main gate of Ajaccio. The Corsican hero died as savagely as he had fought for the island's freedom.

It was in the eighteenth century that Corte became the main stage for Corsica's struggle for independence, particularly in 1755 when Pasquale Paoli declared the town the capital of the newly constituted republic of Corsica. But this last struggle for Corsican independence first broke out in 1729 with Giacinto, Paoli's father, as one of the leaders. This rebellion, first against the Genoese and later against the French, was to last, on and off, for sixty-seven years until the French took permanent possession of the island in 1796. It is the most fascinating period in Corsican history with certain episodes as bizarre and even farcical as others are heroic and memorable in the history of democratic government.

A local revolt broke out near Corte in 1729 when after two disastrous harvests the Genoese ruthlessly pressed claims for taxes. Instantly, the revolt spread across the island, rebel troops encircled Bastia and the Genoese lost control of the interior. Like Sampiero, the new rebel leaders did not belong to seigneurial families nor, indeed, were they the sons of shepherds or peasants. The three men appointed 'Primates' by the assembly held at Corte in 1731 belonged to the new, educated middle-class, fostered ironically by Genoese economic and agricultural policy. Andrea Ceccaldi, Luigi Giafferi and Giacinto Paoli, the chosen leaders, were typical of the new rebels, men from a substantial background who had learned the ways of a wider world while studying law, medicine and theology at Italian universities. But their wealth was modest and the democracy they advocated was based on their own harmonious relationship with the Corsican peasantry.

The Corsicans were united in their desire for independence but, despite the growing weakness of the state of Genoa, the islanders lacked the arms and supplies to support an army strong enough to drive the Genoese out of the island. It was one thing to pass resolutions at assemblies in the safety of Corte and to place the new nation under the protection of the Blessed Virgin of the Immaculate Conception. It was another to force the Genoese into the surrender of their heavily fortified coastal citadels. At first the rebels had some success and captured the small fortresses at St-Florent and Algajola. With the arrival of reinforcements sent by the Emperor Charles VI, the Genoese recaptured these two towns and the rebels were forced into a compromise settlement which made few genuine concessions and left rebellion simmering in the interior of the island.

It will already be apparent that I tend to see Corsica in operatic terms, at times in a serious vein, at others in a lighter mood. We now come to an episode of pure *opéra bouffe*, one of those moments in history which, with hindsight, you can hardly believe that anything so absurd could actually have taken place. The rebellion stumbled on through the early 1730s hindered by a desperate lack of arms and the most basic supplies. Battles were fought and, almost for the lack of boots, lost.

In March 1736, when the rebels must have been near despair, a foreigner of exotic appearance and with a shipload of arms and ammunition landed at Aleria. This was Theodor von Neuhof, one of the more colourful confidence tricksters of the eighteenth century, who, conspiring with certain Greek and Jewish merchants in Tunisia, speculated that Corsica might be ripe for the picking. Encouraged by the sight of a shipload of arms and convincing promises of more to come, the rebels agreed to the impudent request of this adventurer that in return for his support they crown him King of Corsica. Rights of residence were guaranteed to his Tunisian backers and in return he swore an oath to observe the Corsican constitution. His reign lasted eight months. By that time his inept military tactics and a failure to maintain the promised supplies led to massive desertions among the rebel troops and his own ignominious flight over the mountains.

There followed seventeen years of confusion and sporadic fighting. While the rebels attempted by various appointments and assemblies to maintain their government in the interior, the French had already decided to annexe the island. At the request of the Genoese they sent troops to Corsica in 1738 but this force was routed by the rebels. A new French commander arrived in 1739 and defeated the rebel army. The rebel government was in such disarray that about one thousand of the rebel leaders went into exile. They included Giacinto Paoli who fled with his son, Pasquale, to Naples. Seeming to have restored order and suppressed the move for independence, the French troops left the island in 1741.

The French were not the only nation with an eye on Corsica. Britain, in alliance with the Kingdom of Sardinia, had their own plans to partition the island. Under the guise of assisting the rebels, British warships appeared around the Corsican coast, one actually carrying Theodor von Neuhof who can have done nothing to increase the confidence of his former subjects. The British bombardment of Bastia in 1745 was more impressive but the Count Domenico Rivarola, the Sardinian military commander, fell out with Gaffori and the other leaders of the Corsican forces and the armies withdrew from Bastia. In 1748 Bastia was bombarded by the British again and attacked by Sardinian and

Corsican troops. The town was saved by the arrival of French troops. Their commander, the Marquis de Cursay, controlled the island until Genoese intrigue had him removed in disgrace in 1752. The French troops were once again withdrawn at the end of the same year.

Throughout all this disruption of the island's affairs, attempts to establish an independent constitution stumbled on. General Gian'Pietro Gaffori, a doctor from Corte, had become head of state. At another assembly held in October 1752 a new constitution was agreed. But this was not a democratic government since real authority was kept in the hands of the generals and the magistrates. Gaffori himself seems to have abused his power and in 1753 was assassinated in a plot engineered by the Genoese. His place as head of state was taken by a regent council of four which included Clemente Paoli, Pasquale's elder brother. In 1754 Pasquale was invited to return from Naples to Corsica to head the rebels and to establish an independent government. He was at that moment twenty-nine, serving in a Neapolitan regiment in Elba. He accepted the invitation from his countrymen with optimism and a determination to establish Corsica as an independent nation with a democratic government far in advance of its time.

It was to visit Pasquale Paoli that James Boswell landed in Cap Corse in 1765. Although he was only in Corsica for two months, he achieved a considerable friendship with Paoli and spent much time with him. In 1768 he published an account of his adventures and his impressions of Paoli and his proposed form of government in *The Journal of a Tour to Corsica; and Memoirs of Pascal Paoli*. It was Boswell's first book and most successful. A second edition was published in the same year and a third edition, with minor revisions, the following year. The book received enthusiastic reviews. Dr Johnson, however, wrote suggesting that 'I wish you would empty your head of Corsica', while Lord Auchinleck, seeing his son as a dilettante, remarked crushingly that 'Jamie had ta'en a toot on a new horn'. By 1769, in a mellower mood, Johnson wrote to Boswell that 'your Journal is in a very high degree curious and delightful . . . I know not whether I could name any narrative by which curiosity is better excited, or better gratified.' Johnson's revised opinion is an excellent evaluation of the book which still makes interesting reading, not least for its detailed portrait of Paoli and the picture Boswell draws of the life which the rebels lived in and around Corte.

Boswell's first meeting with Paoli did not start well. 'He was polite but very reserved. I had stood in the presence of many a prince, but I have never had such a trial as in the presence of Paoli. I have already said, that he is a great physiognomist. In consequence of his being in continual danger from treachery and assassination, he has formed a habit of studiously observing every new face. For ten minutes we walked backwards and forwards through the room, hardly saying a word, while he looked at me, with a steadfast, keen and penetrating eye, as if he searched my very soul. This interview was for a while very severe upon me. I much was relieved when his reserve wore off, and he began to speak more.'

The fact was that Paoli thought that Boswell was a spy. Years later in London, the exiled Paoli confessed to the company gathered one evening at Mrs Thrale's, 'He came to my country, and he fetched me some letter of recommending him; but I was of the belief he might be an impostor and an espy; for I look away from him, and in a moment I look to him again, and I behold his tablets. Oh! he was to the work of writing down all I say! Indeed, I was angry. But soon I discover he was no impostor and no espy; and I only find I was myself the monster he had come to discern. Oh, (Boswell) is a very good man; I love him indeed; so cheerful! so gay! so pleasant! but at the first, oh! I was indeed angry.' This confession was recorded in Fanny Burney's *Diary*.

Boswell's posturing and inflated prose sometimes make him seem lightweight and sycophantic but all his dealings with Paoli are marked not only by sincere admiration but by boundless loyalty. The *Journal* gives a heroic and noble picture of the Corsican leader but Boswell followed his words by ceaseless efforts on behalf of the Corsicans with the British government and by great kindness to Paoli when he came to London in exile. He lost no time in introducing the Corsican visitor to Dr Johnson, bringing together the two men of virtue whom he most admired.

There is ample historical evidence, even unsupported by Boswell's panegyric, to show that Pasquale Paoli was a distinguished man, cast in that iron mould of Corsican greatness which produced his contemporary and eventual adversary, Napoleon Bonaparte. In the perspective of history Paoli was essentially a man of ideas, Napoleon a man of action, but they are worthy of comparison. The fact that Paoli is long forgotten while Napoleon remains a household word proves little except that the world prefers the drama of battles to the development of political philosophy.

Paoli had a commanding physical presence which impressed Boswell the moment they met. 'I found him alone, and was struck with his appearance. He is tall, strong, and well made; of a fair complexion, a sensible, free, and open countenance, and a manly, and noble carriage. He was then in his fortieth year. He was drest in green and gold. He used to wear the common Corsican habit, but on the arrival of the French he thought a little external elegance might be of use to make the government appear in a more respectable light.' Paoli's character and intellect were equal to his noble appearance. And his exile in Naples with his father had given him the benefit of an excellent university education. He was widely read, a good linguist and with a taste for political philosophy, familiar with the writings of Montesquieu and Rousseau which influenced his development of the new Corsican constitution.

It is significant that even when faced with many great practical problems, in January 1765 he founded a university in Corte, mainly staffed by the Franciscans of the island and with scholarships for poor students. Carlo Bonaparte, Napoleon's father, studied law at the university while acting as a secretary to Paoli. Paoli's liberalism was far in advance of his time. In his own lifetime it was only in America that his attempts to establish a democratic government in Corsica were appreciated. Today, it is easy to find limitations in Paoli's system of democracy. There was much talk of universal suffrage and fair representation in the Diet but in reality Paoli exercised his right to invite certain representa-

13 Fortified citadel high above the fishing port, Bonifacio

14 Ornate tombs at the city of the dead, Bonifacio

15 The great dolmen tomb of Fontanaccia, Sartène

16 Genoese bridge at Spin' A Cavallu, near Sartène

tives of his own choice and, needing the wealth and support of the Church, he allowed them an unequal proportion of seats. Nor, in practice, was his personal, civil or military power controlled by the constitution. Paoli did not always get his own way with the Diet but without doubt on many occasions he exercised an influence on its legislation. Despite such autocratic contradictions to his democratic philosophy there is no doubt all European governments regarded Paoli as an extreme radical. Paoli was also trying to introduce a system of experimental democratic government in a precarious political situation which, like the rebel leaders before him, he lacked the basic means to support. It can be argued that there was a kind of rough and ready democracy latent in Corsican society. It is miraculous that at this disintegrating moment in Corsica's history, Paoli was able to formalise it into a working government.

From the moment on 15 July 1755 when Paoli was elected General of the Nation, he was under attack from the Genoese and the French and in personal danger from various Corsican rivals. He put down two revolts by local families but he was less successful in the main campaign against the French troops brought in at the request of the Genoese in 1759 and 1764. The rebel army lacked supplies, its democratic organisation made it ineffective and Paoli was an indecisive military commander. In May 1768 Genoa ceded the sovereignty of Corsica to France and a year later French troops finally defeated the rebel army at Ponte-Nuovo. France gained control of the island and Paoli was forced to flee into exile to England.

Corsica was ruled by France under the last years of the French monarchy, the administration putting down some further rebellions and offering other rebels amnesties. The French government offered a pardon to Paoli in exile in London but he refused it. After the French Revolution, which was generally welcomed in Corsica, the island was made a part of the French nation and all measures against exiles were repealed. On 17 July 1790 Paoli landed in Bastia receiving a hero's welcome. Two months later at the Congress of Orezza he was elected Commander-in-Chief of the Corsican National Guards and later the President of the island's *Conseil Général*. These harmonious relations with the French authorities were too good to last. By 1793, after the failure of an expedition to capture Sardinia, Paoli was suspected of siding with the British and in April an order was put out for his arrest. The order did nothing but stir up indignation and the Corsican patriots rallied once again in support of Paoli at Corte.

The final phase of Pasquale Paoli's notable career, with the establishment of the bizarre, even somewhat quaint Anglo-Corsican Viceroyalty, moves towards the world of light opera; Strauss if not Gilbert & Sullivan. There was Lady Elliot entertaining the society of Bastia on the lawns of the British residence to garden parties and elegant balls. Meanwhile, the admirable Sir Gilbert was planning a palatial residence built of local marble to be sited in the mountains near Corte.

It was the same story. Despite acclamation from his followers, and confirmation from the national assembly that he was Father of the Nation, Paoli was soon reminded that even a radical democracy must be supported by an effective army and that an army could not protect the nation without adequate supplies. Paoli knew that his situation was desperate. The nation faced an invasion of French troops; ultimately he faced the guillotine. His own troops were without arms or the most basic necessities of life. When the British representative, Sir Gilbert Elliot, landed at Ile-Rousse in January 1794, Paoli was in no position to bargain. Dorothy Carrington pinpoints his predicament where she writes that he accepted whatever Sir Gilbert suggested and implored supplies for his army, 'money, ammunition, biscuits and cheese'.

It was an absurd, 'biscuits and cheese' situation. The British wanted a base in the central Mediterranean and saw no difficulty in manipulating Paoli and his followers to their advantage. Paoli, who had already met Sir Gilbert Elliot in London, felt certain that Britain would supply his needs while not interfering with his democratic government of Corsica. Events were to disillusion both men. It should be said that Sir Gilbert was the best type of British colonial governor, sympathetic to the interests of Corsica and full of enthusiasms for the island. Paoli was unrelenting in his ambition for the independence of Corsica and determined that the alliance with Britain should serve that cause; a cause in which sadly the British government had not the slightest interest.

It was agreed between Elliot and Paoli and proclaimed at an Assembly in Corte in June 1794 that there was to be an Anglo-Corsican kingdom to be ruled over by a Viceroy to be appointed by the British government. Elliot expected that he would be appointed Viceroy. Paoli never doubted that he would be chosen. There was an unfortunate delay of five months in making the announcement. Friction between the two sides increased and rumours were put about that the British were selling out the Corsicans to another foreign power. When the decision finally arrived on 1 October, it did nothing to restore harmony. Sir Gilbert Elliot was appointed Viceroy while Paoli was fobbed off with the promise of a portrait of his new sovereign in a jewelled frame. To make matters worse, Elliot having suggested that the portrait should be presented to Paoli in the form of an official investiture, the wretched picture failed to arrive. The Corsicans, with their characteristic exaggeration in moods of high dudgeon, put it about that Elliot had stolen it.

Elliot, for all his fondness for Corsica, had little understanding of the Corsican character. He was not as sensitive as he should have been to Paoli's disappointment and indignation. He busied himself with setting up the structure of the new government and preparing for the first Parliament which met in Bastia in February 1795. Its first act was to elect Paoli as its President which at one stroke would have undermined the position of the Viceroy. In the strongest terms Elliot informed Parliament that, if Paoli accepted this post, he would immediately withdraw all British troops from the island. It was an effective threat and Paoli immediately refused the Presidency. Elliot had his way but in doing so he lost finally the support of Paoli and his followers. The Corsican rebels had looked to the British for protection, not for government. The British, on the other hand, could not conceive of a British protectorate not ruled over by a British subject.

Elliot, a broad-minded and liberal man judged by the standards of his own time, was incapable of understanding Paoli's political ambitions for Corsica. His attitude, and that of most educated men of that time, is neatly summed up in one of his despatches: 'The ideas expressed in the General's speeches on all political matters are absurd and crude . . . They are, moreover, in direct contradiction to the system of government established here . . . Paoli seems to me to have strong tendencies to democracy. In the 1790s the word 'democracy' summoned up only the worst excesses and freedoms of the French and American revolutions. Paoli was born far in advance of his time. One can hardly blame Elliot for being a man of his own age and an honourable representative of it.

The final act of this drama reached new heights of absurdity. Elliot went on a tour of the south of Corsica which he enjoyed for he loved the wild landscape of the island and the robust life of its villages. But his stay in Ajaccio became the subject of a grotesque accusation that one of his party had deliberately smashed a bust of Paoli during an official ball. Grotesque or not, 'the assassination of the bust', as it came to be called, led to disorder all over the island. As the rioting spread Elliot sat indecisively in Bastia and wrote to London urging that Paoli be recalled into exile. Paoli left Corsica in the autumn and as the situation appeared to quieten down Elliot was convinced that he had solved the problem. But he had lost the sympathy of the rebel forces and eased the way for the return of the French. In September 1796 he received orders to evacuate the island and despite the difficulties he had suffered he left Corsica with great sadness in November. It was typical of the man that he went to great trouble to secure pensions and settle in Italy a number of Corsicans who left with him. Later he became Governor-General of India. When he was created Baron Minto, he included the Moor's head of Corsica in his coat of arms. Paoli lived on in London, a respected member of society, until his death in 1807. He had spent forty-seven years of his life in exile, a life that one must describe as a noble failure.

As you wander through the small squares and the narrow streets of the old town of Corte you may well wonder how all the comings and goings of Paoli's time were fitted in. Strip away the modern part of the town and you are left with hardly more than a substantial village clustered around the citadel. Modern Corte spreads away mostly to the north on either side of the long cours Paoli which has now become the main avenue of the town. Now development is spreading into the outskirts with austere apartment blocks, garages and prefabricated supermarkets; a pattern of urban expansion found all over France. There is, in fact, enough to hold you in and around Corte for at least three days but none of the attractions are in the newer part of the town except for such conveniences as shopping and the post office. The hotels within the town are not to be recommended but we shall come to that intriguing subject in a moment.

At the top of the cours Paoli is the Place Paoli, the main square of Corte and the entrance to the old town or, as the French call it, la ville haute. The small bakers' and grocers' shops around the square are good places for picnic shopping and one or two sell local specialities, the best being thin pasties flavoured with the herbs of the maquis. In the centre of the square is a vacuous bronze statue of Pasquale Paoli, erected in 1854. The French government's recent decision to re-open his university in Corte is a more imaginative memorial to the local hero. The steep ramp running up behind the statue leads to another small square, the Place Gaffori, commemorating the most heroic of the rebel generals. Another bronze statue stands before his house where in 1750 his wife, Faustine, in the absence of her husband, demonstrated the granite resolution of Corsican women. Corte was threatened yet again by the Genoese. When some of the rebel leaders suggested surrender, Madame Gaffori waved a burning torch over a barrel of gunpowder and threatened to blow them all to hell if they spoke again of defeat – 'Choose between death as heroes or cowards!' Corte held out until reinforcements arrived.

At the opposite end of the small square is the Église de l'Annonciation, built around 1450 but much altered in the eighteenth century. Inside is a fine carved wooden pulpit taken from a Franciscan friary; to the left of the choir, the birth certificate of Blaise de Signori, born in 1676. He became a Franciscan and spent many years touring the friaries of the island urging his brothers to return to the primitive rule of prayer and penance. Since the life of the average friar in Corsica was already austere he met with little success but he was canonised as St Theophil in 1930 and is now the patron saint of Corte. Beneath the altar in the side chapel dedicated to him is a deathbed effigy in wax; the kind of devotional tableau I find rather macabre. But the church has a stolid charm, the small belfry rising above the white walls, the building dominating this part of the town, from a distance a counterweight to the mass of the citadel sloping up to the left.

Follow the sloping street up to the Place du Poilu. At No 1, the doorway with a white plaque over it, is the house where the Bonaparte family lived and where Joseph, the eldest son and later King of Spain, was born in 1768, only a few months before the family were forced to flee to Ajaccio. Across the square is Paoli's Palais National which housed his Parliament and his administration and, from 1765, the new university. The small size of the building and its lack of grandeur – squeezed between the backstreets and the base of the citadel – remind one of the courage and hopelessness of Paoli's cause. It was a republic on a shoestring. It might have worked if Corsica had been left to its own democratic devices. The real tragedy of Corsica was its commanding position in the western Mediterranean. Paoli might have driven out the Genoese but his ill-equipped, undisciplined army had no chance against the great powers of Europe. These sad remains of his capital conjure up a noble but unrealisable dream.

The citadel has splendid views over the town and the surrounding countryside and mountains but in itself is a gloomy place. Near the entrance are two large and later barrack blocks which must have been in use until recently. Now, with broken windows and shattered doors, they seem to have been vandalised. Higher up thick stone walls rise sheer from their rocky foundations to form a complex circle of fortifications. On arrival at the top via narrow flights of steps one wonders what they were protecting. The citadel is crowned with a few derelict buildings more like small barns than military installations. On the terraces just below are rows of grim prison cells, windowless and comfortless, with bunks built from blocks of stone. Behind the citadel, the mountains rise steeply, in autumn their arid flanks sweeping up to the purple heights. Below, to the south, is a platform flattened out among leaning slabs of rock, the Belvédère and the viewpoint to the meeting-place 100 m below of the Tavignano and the Restonica rivers. It is a fine view looking towards the mouth of the Restonica gorge but building on this edge of the town is spoiling it.

Despite what I have written about Corte, some of which must seem disparaging, I like the town, both for itself and because it is a good centre for a number of exciting excursions into the surrounding mountains and countryside. The first time I came to Corte I stayed only one day and thought it a drab little town. It was more dreary in those days and I doubt if I appreciated its heroic place in Corsican history. The second time we stayed four days and, apart from marvellous excursions, we enjoyed the town. It does not stand examination building by building but for any visitor wandering through the steep lanes of the old town it has a rugged charm. The October sun threw great patterns of light and shade across the streets and up the pocked faces of the houses. At the top of a cobbled flight of steps the statue of Gaffori declaimed before the stained pink plaster of another house. In another direction the cobbled lane led into the sunshine, fruit was piled high before a grocer's shop and over a low stone wall trees framed the view to the mountains. One moment the view within the town is sombre, the next picturesque. It is a charm of the place that will only be discovered by unhurried and aimless wandering.

That is not the only charm of Corte. Whatever you do, spend at least one night at the Auberge de la Restonica. That October, we arrived late in Corte. We stayed the night in a gloomy but comfortable hotel in the centre of the new town. Since we intended to stay in Corte for another three nights I was keen to stay in quieter and more attractive surroundings. I saw that the *Guide Bleu* listed a hotel 'à l'entrée des Gorges de la Restonica' with the intriguing rating of one star for the hotel and two for the restaurant. It sounded exactly our kind of place and we set off across the Pont Tavignano and down a long street of crumbling houses and dusty trees. Soon the town was behind us and we were on a rough track with the Restonica river glinting through the trees well below us to left. A few more kilometres and there was the sign to the hotel pointing down a steep drive to the left.

The large car park was empty and the windows of the hotel were shuttered. It looked a most attractive place but deserted. Even the menu cards in a frame by the door looked like last summer's and had it not been for the bark of a dog on the other side of the house I might have turned away. Encouraged by this sign of life I tried the door and it opened. We entered and found ourselves in a large hall which ran up through two storeys with a surrounding gallery. The place was gloomy but not unoccupied. The dining room ran off to the right and the great hall was overfurnished with sofas and armchairs. Each one was occupied by an old gentleman, breathing noisily but fast asleep. Well, not exactly old gentlemen but a variety of large dogs, stretched out like clubmen after an indulgent lunch. The largest were extended on the sofas, their paunchy, bald stomachs rising and falling in the rhythms of digestion and contentment. Two or three smaller dogs were napping comfortably in the large armchairs, their dreams and nightmares sending occasional vibrations through their limbs. I had read occasionally of hotels for dogs but had never envisaged anything quite as delightful as this. But it did leave me wondering where we should fit in.

At that moment a churlish young woman appeared and, ignoring the dogs, told us that there were rooms vacant and booked us in. We had a pleasant room which looked out over the large garden at the back of the hotel. To the left about one-third of the garden had been fenced off to form a large pen, full of small buildings, sheds, wired enclosures and dogs. Although we stayed three days I never succeeded in counting how many though I did one morning reach a total of twenty-five cats. This spotless animal kingdom was ruled over by a statuesque, elderly woman with wild grey hair and a flowing white robe. She was aided by two gnomic men, whose kibbutz hats gave them an air of 'Bill and Ben, the Flowerpot Men', those favourites of children's television many years ago. They also moved about the garden with that same aimless purposefulness of B and B, making long, hobbling journeys right across the garden only to return laden with one nail. I spent a lot of time at the bedroom window during our stay.

All was revealed at breakfast next morning which we had on the terrace overlooking the garden. We got into conversation with 'the Woman in White' who turned out to be the owner and most charming. The whole thing had been unintentional she explained. She loved dogs and a few years before a friend in the town had brought her a dog which she had found cruelly neglected. The word went round Corte and in no time our hostess found she was running a home for stray and ill-treated dogs. The cats came of their own accord and she had never attempted to count them. She told us one or two stories about cases of cruelty and said that few people cared. An insistent barking from the compound interrupted us and Madame swept away to give her charges breakfast leaving behind a small white rascal with a large black patch over one eye who begged disarmingly for lumps of sugar the moment his mistress was out of sight.

It was the triumph of Madame that when guests were staying in the hotel they were never troubled by the dogs or the cats. Even more remarkable, the animals were so well looked after, I never once detected the smell of cat or dog during our stay. If all these pleasures and amusements were not enough, the food and wine in the restaurant were excellent and one night I had a stew of wild boar which was the most tender game meat I have ever tasted. In every way the auberge makes a perfect base for enjoying Corte and its surroundings but it is small and in or out of season, anyone intending to stay there should telephone and make a booking. We arrived early in the day and by the evening the hotel looked full.

There are a number of excursions you can make from Corte, all of them worthwhile. To the west and north-west lie the greatest mountains of Corsica and in this area you should not miss the Gorges de la Restonica; further north, the Scala di Sta Regina which is the gateway to the magnificent route to Porto and, most northerly, the spectacular Gorges de l'Asco. Asco and Restonica can each be visited from Corte in one day. When you have finished with Corte you can continue your tour to Porto enjoying the scenery on your way, again a comfortable one-day drive. It is only a short drive from Corte north to Ponte Leccia and from there you can explore the chestnut forests of La Castagniccia. On the drive back to Corte from Ponte Leccia I enjoyed the less dramatic but charming countryside to the east of the main road, following the D 39 and D 15 through Bustanico and Sermano and returning to Corte along the last few kilometres of the N 200. In the remainder of this chapter I am going to describe the Gorges de la Restonica, saving the other mountain drives for later chapters where they will have their appropriate settings.

The scenery around the entry to the gorges hardly hints at the wild splendour ahead. The Restonica river tumbles along its rocky bed below the sloping hillside and through the quiet woodland. Quite soon the narrow road starts to twist and turn. The pine forest thickens and, cradled in the green frame of their branches is the first view of the towering bastions and pinnacles of granite, a massive fortress of rock rising in the middle distance with other lines of peaks beyond. It is a harsh landscape but the simple, subdued colouring is beautiful. The vast sky is totally blue except for one cotton-white cloud resting along a distant ridge. The enormous space of the sky adds height to the craggy outline of mountains, the granite blurred in mixture of purple shadow and pink-grey faces and falls of scree bright in the direct sunlight. Further into the gorges the trees are sparser allowing the silhouette of each leaning pine a character of its own, their greens the more precious against the background of harsh white scree patched with brown grasses. Where the road runs out, one feels one has travelled through a new world. In reality, it is only 15 km from Corte to the Bergeries de Grotelle. The compression of Corsica gives it its own scale of height and distance.

One is in the heart of the mountains here. To the right is Capo au Chiostro rising to 2295 m and to the left the Rotondo reaching a height of 2622 m. It is a world of granite. All around, rising out of the falls of scree, are steep, rough-faced cliffs, drawn out against the sky in ragged buttresses and towering spires of rock. To one side of the gorge huddle a group of shepherds' old, drystone refuges, long disused. Except for one, where an enterprising man from Corte has adapted a group of these buildings to form a café and a summer home for himself. There was little trade in October and he was just about to close for the winter. The café and his quarters were cave-like, curious and neat as a ship's cabin. He served us excellent coffee and, standing trim and handsome as a greying film star, showed us souvenirs of the mountains, the skins of animals and the like and, with special pride, the postcards he had received from visitors to his café from all over the world. In the centre of the room an icy stream trickled from the rocks into a pool crammed with bottles. It was his refrigerator. He had been running the café for fifteen years, staying alone in the gorge between May and October. In the winter months he returned to Corte where he worked as a butcher making charcuterie. When it was time to go, I tried to pay for our coffee. He refused. He had invited us in and we were his guests.

From this place where the road ends you can walk on along good paths to the Melo lake (1h 15) and beyond to the Capitello lake (2h). Melo is the source of the Restonica river. It is a beautiful walk with dramatic views of the mountains on either side and the water of the Restonica reflecting the blue of the sky between its banks of flat granite boulders. In autumn, among the rocks and nesting amidst clumps of dry grasses were tiny cyclamen, more like pink butterflies fluttering on patches of green moss. If you do not have the energy to walk to the lakes you will find plenty to please you in the immediate landscape around the shepherds' old huts. And in spring and autumn you are likely to have the place and all its magnificence to yourself.

8

A Fantasy Coast

PORTO

From the first moment that I saw the small fishing village of Porto it cast some kind of spell over me and remained in my mind as the most romantic place in Corsica. There is no logic in this process but certain places drop like a stone into one's imagination causing the ripples of memory to widen until recollection may bear little relation to reality. Since that first arrival in May 1963, I have often day-dreamed of Porto; standing in trains, lying sleepless in bed, conjuring up for my renewed pleasure the harbour, the eucalyptus wood and those rising crags of pink granite that threaten the sky. Each time it became more perfect, its features creating in my memory a fantasy coast.

As we drove down the last steep stretch of road on my return to Porto in 1986 I felt nervous. To the traveller old dreams are precious. I wondered how reality would match up to my memories and, a greater hazard, how reality itself had stood up to the tourist invasion. I do believe in certain miracles. Apart from a few new hotels near the harbour Porto was as beautiful as ever and, in October, as deserted as it had been in 1963. Our quaint hotel – le Soleil Couchant – was still there, tucked in a corner above the quay. The rooms and plumbing remained simple but the rock platform in front had been transformed into a pleasant terrace-restaurant. Madame was noticeably older, her smile more like a sour lemon than ever. Her husband hovered between eccentricity and senility and viewed us throughout our stay with the gravest suspicion. He had become totally deaf so I never discovered in what sinister rôle we had been cast in his failing mind. He kept an eye on me as if I was about to steal the cutlery off the tables, always laid well in advance of lunch and dinner and, at this late season, usually unoccupied.

It is not history or architecture that have made Porto such a famous resort. It is its magnificent position, encircled by cliffs and mountains with the serene Golfe de Porto spreading away from the harbour to the horizon. Porto's character is composed of unusual qualities of light and colour. The reflections and patterns of sunlight and shade give life to the rock, the water and the strange forest of eucalyptus behind the beach. These contribute to the mood of the place. Above all else, it is the surrounding granite which gives Porto its unique and dramatic beauty. Out to sea ragged promontories and steep capes rise from the placid water. Inland, cliffs and hills rise behind the town ascending to spires and pinnacles of granite towering against the sky. It is a world of rock; rugged, hard and barren yet of unforgettable beauty.

The rock formations alone are memorable, in dramatic contrast with the gently rippled sea or the still blue of the sky. But beyond everything there are the extraordinary colours of the granite, colours which are never static or precise, changing at each hour of the day. In the hard morning light there are drab greys, beige to sand-brown and a tawny orange. When the light and the shadows soften in the afternoon, a range of pinks appear, lit seemingly from within, turning in the mist of dusk to blurred purple and violet. Later, in the incandescent sunset which sends an orange fire across the waters of the gulf, the rocks turn black but they do not die. Their outlines remain sharp and dramatic to the last second of total darkness. This area around Porto – down from the Gorges de Spelunca, north out to Capo Cenino and south to the cliffs of les Calanche – is one of the most spectacular rock-landscapes in the world.

The most dramatic approach to Porto is by the narrow but magnificent road (D 84) from Corte which, nearly all the way, offers impressive views of great mountains, forests, rivers and lakes; among the finest drives in the island. You are soon amidst the awe-inspiring chaos of rock, known as the Scala di Santa Regina. One can see the lines of old mule-tracks which once clung to the sheer cliffs above the Golo river. A slip of the foot must have cost many men and their beasts their lives in this fierce landscape. Further on is the Calacuccia damn with a long lake beyond. From the south side you look across the water and up the opposite slopes to a superb panorama of Corsica's high mountains. The tallest, Monte Cinto, rises in the middle to 2710 m. On along through the increasingly mountainous landscape, the road climbs and falls through the cool shade of the Forêt de Valdo-Niello and the Forêt d'Aitone. At the Col de Vergio the view spreads out over the pine forest, the air chilly and freshened by the slight scent of resin. These are the tall Corsican pines which Nelson coveted for his ships' masts.

After the small town of Evisa the road narrows again and twists down in a frenzy of bends hurtling you towards the Gorges de Spelunca, the first great spectacle in this kingdom of granite magnificence. Through the fringe of trees at the roadside one looks straight down into the depths of the gorge enclosed by striated walls of granite, orange to the right, greyer to the left; brushed here and there with green undergrowth. One thousand metres below the Porto river draws a crystal line through the maquis along the base of the gorge. At the end of the vista formed by the side walls of the gorge a battlement of granite spreads across the horizon. Capo d'Ota stands among a cluster of sharp peaks commanding the far end of the gorge. It is backed by steep, broken ridges, a scarred façade to the massive wall of granite along the skyline. The haze of the sunlight blurs the distant pinks into blues and the blues into a mist of purple, hardly more than long shadows between the deep folds of the rock. The Gorges de Spelunca is the perfect gateway to Porto, opening the mind to the extraordinary subtleties of the landscapes that lie ahead.

I came both times to Porto along this road. The second time, eager for another view of Spelunca, we lingered above the gorge, stopping several times along the road to enjoy this upper view from different angles; 100 m or more down the road give you surprisingly different views. I did not on either occasion descend into the gorge and enjoy what must be the superb views there, following the road from Porto to the old village of Ota. Even enjoying the views from the heights of the main road we did not arrive in Porto until the late afternoon. After settling in the hotel and a stroll around the town, it was time for a lengthy dinner and bed.

At breakfast on the terrace the next morning I had intended to read my guide-books and make a plan for the day. The French couple at the next table distracted me from my maps. There are moments when the human scene can distract from the most alluring landscape. They quarrelled without pause. The wife, suitably, had a face cut out of granite, the stark lines centring on stern, accusing eyes. The husband was dapper, additionally hiding his inadequacies behind a greying Van Dyke beard. He stroked it with an assumed complacency. He looked so neat and controlled in his lemon shirt and grey shorts. The opening bone of contention was the shirt. It was the wrong shirt, not the one that his wife had laid out for him. The shirt took a bitter fifteen minutes, two croissants and large cups of coffee. Unbelievably, and with some solemnity, after breakfast they took each other's photographs. She stood erect by the table with the authority of a petty official. Monsieur fluffed up the edges of his beard and posed himself with care on the plastic chair. I wondered which of them kept the family photograph album and pondered on the wisdom of never trying to understand other people's marriages, friends or total strangers.

Porto is divided by a promontory of rock surmounted by the square, squat ruins of an ancient Genoese fort, most notable as the best viewing point for the sunset across the gulf. The old fishing port crouches under the northern face of the promontory, the short quay now devoid of fishing boats but surrounded by small hotels and the commerce of tourism. Across the water, beyond the largest hotel – a white and obtrusive structure of terraces and bedroom balconies – is a factory which makes easily resistible objects of mother-of-pearl. Happily, little other activity disturbs the mellow atmosphere of October. We wandered up through the small town, a few shops but mostly hotels and restaurants jostling for the view. We crossed the ridge of the promontory and below was the lovely second half of the town.

At the foot of the tumbling orange rocks, the Porto river narrowed away from its mouth under a curving iron bridge to disappear between flat spits of pebbles into the shadows of the overhanging trees. Across the river a stony beach spread in a sweeping arc across the floor of the gulf to the soft green slopes beyond. Soft slopes that rose swiftly to cliffs of pink granite and beyond to the pinnacles and walls of the mountains that divided the town from the sky. Just below the bridge, curving with oriental serenity, a group of fishing boats swam in the river, secured by ropes to the rocks. The fishing fleet of Porto seemed to have shrunk to no more than a cluster of long, open dinghies, heavy with nets and oars, brightly coloured and canopied but now anchored on the wrong side of the promontory.

On the old quay of Porto we saw only the tourist excursion boats, manned, not by fishermen, but by tour operators and hippies. We had signed on for the tour to the famous nature reserve and bird sanctuary, La Scandola, and our boat was due to leave Porto at 9.30 in the morning. The white cruiser was there punctually but its tourist activities were to a slight extent subsidised by coastal trading. We had to wait patiently while some heavy goods were off-loaded and a small tractor was manoeuvred ashore along two narrow, trembling planks. Cargo safe on the quay, the passengers boarded supervised by the crew of three, none of them resembling the normal image of a seaman. We might just as well have set to sea in charge of the Walrus and the Carpenter. Looking back, the Scandola tour did have certain absurdities which would not have been out of place in a nautical chapter of *Alice in Wonderland*. At the moment when I bought the tickets I knew that it would be something of a 'frost' but I have an appetite for that kind of frolic. As we speeded out of Porto our captain was at the helm. He did have a commanding presence and vanity that bristled from his trim beard and his tanned, elegant legs. A brief spell at the wheel established his rôle as commander of the boat but the act of steering in calm waters soon palled and he handed over to his number two while he went aft to make sure that his passengers were happy. In fact, he devoted the next thirty minutes to chatting-up the prettiest girl aboard and never exchanged a word with the rest of us.

The second member of the crew was a nondescript young man

who did most of the work. The third member did nothing. He had a melancholy face and his sidewhiskers and dank, balding hair gave him the air of some minor character in a Dickens' novel. He brought on board with him a greasy bag which I had presumed were tools. This was placed carefully at his feet when he took up his position leaning over the partition which separated the passengers from the wheelhouse. He occupied himself with staring into space with an occasional burst of activity when he burrowed amongst his sidewhiskers with a dirty finger-nail, peering with interest at the results of these forays. He must have been burning up more energy than I thought for at regular intervals he plunged into the greasy bag for refreshment: tins of beer punctuated by ragged sandwiches which he stuffed into his mouth with gusto. He had an insatiable appetite. During our only stop I saw him make for the nearest café to replenish his tool kit. Perhaps some French regulation demanded a crew of three on a boat of this size and this layabout came cheaper than a more active deckhand.

We were off and the large motor launch ran smoothly northwest across the Golfe de Porto to Capo Cenino. It was a perfect day, a high, cloudless sky and the sun already hot. Above the northern point of the gulf, Monte Cenino rose in a pyramid of granite, the orange rock afire with an inner heat. The boat moved on into the Golfe de Girolta and in front of us rose the wild promontory of La Scandola, recently created as a nature reserve for bird and plant life. It is so strictly protected that members of the public are not allowed to land. The steep, eroded cliffs are the nesting ground of gulls, cormorants and the rare sea-eagles. Over the face of the rock, amongst the clumps of maquis, some rare plant life flourishes. Great white splashes of guano across the nesting cliffs proved that at certain seasons La Scandola must be alive with birds. We saw only a few gulls and cormorants and high up among the crags two or three deserted eyries of the sea-eagles. It was one of many occasions in Corsica when I wished that I had brought a pair of binoculars since from a boat the life on La Scandola is remote.

There is plenty, apart from the bird life, to make this boat tour worthwhile. Within the small area around La Scandola there is a fascinating variety of granite formations and, underwater, magical colour where the boat eases its way into the deep coves and creeks of the cliffs. Here porphyry lies over a granite base and volcanic action and centuries of erosion by wind and water have in turn produced a strange variety of formations and rock sculpture. On the north side of La Scandola I saw a peculiar rock formation that I have seen only once before, on the tiny Pacific island of Ponape. At some early geological stage the rock had been formed into bundles of long, perfectly formed rectangular pillars. In Ponape an early civilisation had used them to build an elaborate ceremonial structure. Here, they lay submerged just beneath the sea or joined to the cliff wall, giving the impression of an abandoned stonemasons' yard. In Ponape, where they had been removed from their natural setting, I took it for granted that those perfect pillars had been fashioned by men.

In the narrow coves the water took on mysterious colours with crusted pink coral formations clinging to the rock and, below, a bed of white sand showing up the shapes and shades of shells and trembling underwater plants. The water had a wonderful clarity in the shade of the rock chimney reaching above us. Then the boat turned into the open bay, the sun struck down and all the colours changed, the depths disappearing under the glittering surface. It did not compare with the tropical underwater world of Ponape but it was beautiful enough.

Having described the pleasures of this boat trip so far, you may be wondering why I started by being so scathing about it. I might have been less severe had I not been led to expect one of the most important bird sanctuaries in southern Europe. I could have forgiven the scarcity of birds had it not been announced just as the boat seemed to be heading back for Porto that we were going to be landed at Girolta for four hours where we might have lunch and swim. Girolta merits half an hour, it was far too cold to swim and like 'old sidewhiskers' we had our own provisions. I had been puzzled from the start why the tour took so long but I had thought that we should be landing for a walk on La Scandola. But it's always the same, all around the world. Bus tour or boat tour, each gets padded out with a long and boring stop where you are urged to eat in an expensive restaurant or buy in expensive shops. As the Scrooge of the organised tour, it never fails to irritate me.

The only unusual fact about the small port of Girolta is that it is virtually inaccessible except by sea. There is a rough track several kilometres across country to the nearest road but its real lines of communication and supply are by boat. The small port is sheltered by a promontory of rock which accommodates a restaurant at one end and the inevitable Genoese tower at the other. Half the beach is occupied by wooden quays reaching out into the water; the other half providing a scruffy swimming area. I had inspected everything to my own satisfaction in fifteen minutes. I retired to sulk for the next three hours in a beachside café with a beer and an endearing old donkey who kept examining me through the geraniums growing along the wall. In that he looked as bored as I felt, I found him most sympathetic. He also had a splendid sharp-edged bray which frightened the life out of the three enormously fat Corsican ladies seated at the next table. That helped to pass the time until the boat left and we sailed around the point and across the bay to Porto with a perfect view of the mountains rising up immediately behind the port.

Late in the afternoon I went for a walk in the shade of the eucalyptus forest in the valley behind the town. It fills the gap between the slopes on cither side with a dense, dusty greenness and gives this landscape an exotic look. During the last century or more Australia has sent its national tree around the world. The gum is adaptable and fast growing and has taken root and flourished in the most unlikely places. But removed from its Australian setting, these tall, dusty trees always look slightly out of place. I think it was the unexpected sight of the eucalyptus wood that helped to fix Porto in my memory. Standing tall and feathery against the sharp outline of the pink granite mountains, they are out of place but have the charm of surprise adding to Porto's dreamlike character. In autumn the trees are covered with small nuts which, from a distance, look like silver-white flowers. Looking through the lines of tall, dappled trunks, the long leaves trailing in festoons of silver-green and starred with white pods with the peaks in the distance, it is a magic scene.

We were hungry that evening and decided to try a restaurant across the port which looked attractive and offered a good menu. The *salade niçoise* was hardly in front of me when a black kitten jumped up into the empty chair beside mine and with an instant mewing started to scratch my arm for his share. A small, yapping dog appeared under our table and began snapping at the kitten. It was not the atmosphere in which to enjoy dinner. Madame, who was obviously the fond owner of the animals, stood near our table, immobile and indifferent. She was statuesque in a tight green skirt, green sweater and shoes and her hair bound up in a construction of green bands of shiny plastic with a spray or two of green feathers. By now the scrap between cat and dog had developed into a running war between our legs, enlivened with lots of mewing, yapping and barking. I struggled on for a little with the salad but it seemed to have lost its savour. After the kitten had plunged its claws into my leg for the third time and the dog, now frenzied, had caused the whole table to vibrate, I turned and summoned Madame. She swung round slightly – a movement from her elegant hips and about as far as the skirt would allow – gave me one of those chilling glances that only her kind can give and swung back to her contemplation of the street.

'Madame,' I asked with all the iciness that I could muster, 'are you running a restaurant here or a zoological garden? Please make up your mind since I'm on the verge of leaving without paying.'

My iciness was wasted on her but French women of her kind know all about *paying*. She did not hurry herself but at her own tight-skirted pace she withdrew to the restaurant kitchen. Two minutes later she returned carrying two small dishes, the animals' meal. With calculated scorn she set down these offerings immediately in front of our table. They were not an attractive sight but they restored peace. Game, set and match to Madame. We choked down the rest of our meal and I paid the bill.

I have one last excursion from Porto to recommend, a beautiful drive to the south ending up at the most unusual and attractive village of Cargèse. It is only 31 km either way although it will seem more with the first section of precarious coast road but it is one of those routes on which you are rewarded for returning along the same road. It is true of many of the mountain roads in Corsica but particularly driving through les Calanche, with the result that coming and going you enjoy two entirely different views. The road climbs up out of the river valley of Porto, crosses the bridge in the small upper village and climbs again to the cliffs above the gulf. Before long one is driving through a striking landscape of pink and orange granite, on the seaward side forming a line of angry granite teeth. The rough pinnacles of rock descend in rows amongst the trees and maquis. It is another world of tortured, thrusting, burning-coloured rock formations, ragged, elongated shoulders intermingled with sharp needles and bastions like castle walls. Please do not hurry, coming or going. Many parking places have been carved out of the rock. Take advantage of them for they were carefully chosen, each offering a different view and marvellous opportunities for photography. And in certain lights the view over the Golfe de Porto is bright and sharp. The trees in the foreground are green, leaf by leaf, the sea like rippled glass, and the distant beaches and falling promontories sharply defined and bright in oranges and pinks. Even the soft white clouds resting on the last line of mountains are precisely shaped against the flat sky. At other times one seems to look down on two divided worlds. The trees make a black frame for the sharp, burning crenellations of the rocks while behind another world floats softly in a purple mist, peaks of granite floating insubstantially in this pall of dense light. Les Calanche beggars description and is one of the greatest marvels of the Corsican landscape.

On the northern edge of the Golfe de Sagone, nesting above the sea, is the quaint village of Cargèse. It would be unknown and unvisited had it not been for some 200 Greeks, who were settled here by the French in 1774 and who, in the mid-nineteenth century, built a Greek Orthodox church which is prettily sited across a small valley immediately opposite the Roman Catholic church. The arrival of a colony of Greek refugees goes back some time before that. In the late seventeenth century some Greeks, fleeing from the Turkish occupation, negotiated with the Genoese a grant of land in Corsica, in a village called Paomia, near Vico. About 600 Greeks settled there in 1676 and, planting vines, fruit and olive trees, made it into a prosperous area. In time they aroused the jealousy of the local Corsicans who attacked the colony in 1715 and again in 1729. In 1732 the Greeks were forced to take refuge in Ajaccio where they were given new land and built a chapel on the western outskirts of the town which still exists.

After the French had taken possession of Corsica, they gave the remaining Greeks the village of Cargèse to compensate for the loss of Paomia, and Marbeuf had 120 houses and a small church built for them. After they had been resettled there the colony was attacked and, in 1793, burnt, forcing the Greeks to return to Ajaccio. But by the end of the century they were firmly established in Cargèse and succeeded in making peace with their Corsican neighbours. An unusual harmony was created between the two communities which is symbolised by the close siting of the two churches. The present Greek church was built between 1852 and 1870, a heavy building crowned by an unusual octagonal tower. On the terrace around the church grow Argentinian nettle-trees with massive trunks planted here in 1898. The interior of the Greek church in a glance carries you east across the Mediterranean. Candles burn before the heavily decorated iconstasis which separates the sanctuary from the nave and to the left is an old icon of St John the Baptist, said to have been painted by a monk on Mount Athos, and brought to Corsica by the original Greek colonists. Across the small valley, the Latin church is also attractive and well kept. The old jealousies died years ago and today the two communities are so close to each other that mass is celebrated alternately in each church, the whole community celebrating both the Latin and the Eastern rite. The two churches even share one choir.

On the drive back to Porto stop on the road above the village of Piana, typical of the picturesque Corsican village spread out on a hillside, the houses clustered around the white church, their orange roofs set off by the green of the orchards and vines lining the slopes behind and, in the distance, the pink granite of les Calanche which lie a kilometre or two ahead. And when you are once again surrounded by these distinctive rock formations, enjoy the reverse view and, in particular, looking over the top of these sharp ramparts down onto the blue calm of the Golfe de Porto across to the headland of La Scandola in the distance. I can only hope that your own recollections of this fantasy coast, more colour than substance, will weave dreams in your memory.

9

The Faithful Citadel

CALVI AND THE NORTH-WEST

In Calvi the summer holiday mood lingered on into late October. On the quayside lunchtime cutlery and glasses made a festive rattle in the shade of the broad palm trees growing between the awnings of the restaurants. Climbing the flights of steps within the citadel, orange bougainvillea and blue plumbago brightened the decaying walls. On a patch of waste ground between the ramparts six neglected kittens lazed in the heat or stalked each other through the weeds. If I were a summer visitor, I would come to Calvi. It is the most attractive resort town in Corsica. It has character, interest and life and a crescent of fine beach curving south around the gulf. Tourism has been better controlled here than anywhere else in the island. The authorities have chosen quality rather than quantity. It is the visitor who benefits from the strict building regulations and the other local laws which preserve the old town, its port and its whole environment.

The citadel of Calvi ranks with those of Bonifacio and Bastia, both for its magnificent site and its impressive martial architecture. Rising on the point at the end of the town, it overlooks the gulfs to the east and the west and cradles the old port beneath the eastern ramparts. The ramparts on this side link three massive bastions, their granite walls sloped and sharply faceted. The bulk of the fortifications rise above Calvi like a truncated mountain. Above the walls, the tall, white houses of the old town rise up, adding a further precarious storey to a structure which, from the quay, seems to fill the sky. I think the general scale and proportions are more effective than Bonifacio. On several terrible occasions the inhabitants and the fortifications of both old and new town proved themselves equally resistant to siege.

From as early as the fifth century BC the Golfe de Calvi was probably used as a port by the Phoenicians, the Greeks and the Etruscans. By the first century the Romans had established a trading port here called 'Sinus Caesiae' and in the last days of the Roman occupation a Christian basilica was built in the town. The Roman settlement was destroyed by the Vandals and the Ostrogoths but in the eleventh to thirteen centuries, under Pisan protection, Calvi was rebuilt as a small port. The citadel and the old town date from the second half of the thirteenth century and the struggle for power between the most powerful Corsican seigneurs. Giovanninello of Nebbio built the first citadel in 1268 but ten years later the people of Calvi rebelled against the tyrannical Corsican masters and in 1278 sought the protection of the Genoese. The Republic saw that Calvi offered the same strategic advantages as Bonifacio and, anxious to ensure the lasting loyalty of Calvi, they granted the town the same tax exemptions and other privileges already given to Bonifacio. It was a wise investment. Until the Genoese handed Corsica over to France in the eighteenth century, the people of Calvi remained unfailingly loyal to Genoa. The dramatic repulse of the King of Aragon by Bonifacio is matched by the courage of Calvi when in 1553 they twice withstood the attack of the French supported by the Turkish fleet. The women of the town fought as fiercely as the men and at the end of the siege the breaches in the walls were blocked by the dead, wives by their husbands. This victory earned Calvi its famous motto, *Civitas Calvi semper fidelis*. That invincible good faith continued to the eighteenth century when Paoli, denied the support of Calvi, was forced to build l'Ile-Rousse in 1758 as his own port on the west coast. When Paoli returned from exile at the end of the century, his brief alliance with the British saw the final defeat of Calvi. British troops and a British fleet subjected the town to a terrible bombardment. It was a historic engagement. The citadel of Calvi was reduced to a ruin and Lord Nelson lost his eye.

Below the entrance to the citadel a large square separates the old town from the new town and the port. This is the Place Christophe-Colomb, the name supporting a dubious tradition that the great navigator was born here. High up in the old town you will find a house marked as his birthplace but you will find a number of other birthplaces in towns in Italy and in Spain. Dorothy Carrington laments the fact that in its enthusiasm to adopt Columbus, without a shred of historical evidence, they have ignored a genuine son, different but equally famous. Although Miguel Manara, later to be nicknamed Don Juan, was born in Seville in 1627, he was the son of Corsican parents who had moved there from Calvi. When the boy was eight his father wished to enrol him in the exclusive order of the Knights of Calatrava and with the help of the Genoese authorities produced evidence of his families' noble Corsican ancestry.

The real Don Juan has become confused in popular imagination with the romantic hero of Molino's play *El Burlador de Sevilla*, the source for further brilliant romanticising by Molière, Mozart, Byron and others. Miguel Manara saw the Spanish play in 1641 and it is said that it immediately inspired in him a determination to lead a life of endless seduction. But, as Dorothy Carrington emphasises, there was nothing romantic in this or in his sexual licence. It was the decision of an arrogant Corsican deliberately choosing a life of crime. The end is even stranger than the beginning and probably as little known as Don Juan's Calvi origins. Miguel Manara repented late in life and died in sanctity. The Vatican initiated the proceedings for canonisation and Manara was accorded the title of Venerable, the first step to sainthood. Calvi, for one reason or another, has forgotten this famous son and you will search in vain for the house of the Manara family. Nor is the association mentioned in the French guide-books.

The Place Christophe-Colomb, for all its unhistorical associations, is now little more than a spacious car park. Facing the main street there is a melodramatic war memorial commemorating the First World War, all bronze and white sugar-icing marble, in a style which the French have made peculiarly their own; an overt sentimentality in direct contradiction to their usual rational character. British war memorials belong more suitably to the 'stiff upper lip' school of sculpture; a granite pillar with a neat list of names on a bronze plaque. Imagine some tidy village green in Surrey with a bronze soldier dying in his mother's arms at the edge of the green. It really wouldn't do at all; like crying at the funeral.

The citadel rises up on the east side of the square; its walls, as the *Guide Bleu* nicely puts it, the colour of a ewes' milk cheese. The only entrance is well fortified with a drawbridge and portcullis and over the gate are the arms of Calvi and its celebrated motto. By the entrance is the old Palais des Gouverneurs génois, originally built in the thirteenth century and enlarged in 1554 by the Office of St George when they took over control of the island and renovated a number of the old citadels. Dominating the centre of the town is the church of Saint Jean-Baptiste. It was first built in the thirteenth century but badly damaged when the nearby arsenal exploded and was rebuilt in 1577. It was made the cathedral in 1576. There are a number of interesting paintings in the church together with two fine fonts and a painted pulpit. Several of these works of art are closely associated with the history of the town. It is said that the Turks raised their siege in 1553 when a painting of *Christ des Miracles* was brought out onto the ramparts.

The real pleasure of the citadel is to be found in wandering up and down its narrow streets and enjoying the views of the bays on either side of the town walking around the ramparts. The great views across the sparkling expanse of the sea make a pleasing contrast to the cramped town and shadowy lanes, cobbles breaking into flights of steps. I enjoyed each shabby detail, a decrepit roofline with crazy chimney pots rising drunkenly from the old tiles, a pristine sea behind the house pointing up its charming decrepitude. At the top of one flight of steps a great Ali Baba terracotta jar, a spiky plant shooting out of it as if Struwwelpeter were crouched inside. The house behind was festooned by a particularly long and interesting line of washing. These trophies of intimate life do encourage the voyeur instinct in one and the occasional garment defeats the wildest imagination. But after living for several years in the oriental world I have learned that there is as much cultural difference in underclothes, particularly male, as in art and architecture.

Back on the quay of the old port, there is nothing of importance but everything is delightful. Occasionally, it is a relief to know that one can put one's guide-book in one's pocket and simply wander at will, examining the menus of attractive-looking restaurants identifying unusual vegetables outside the general store or just watching men unload crates of beer. Calvi encourages this sense of irresponsibility and perhaps that is why I enjoyed it so much. There is a street just behind the quay, the Rue Clemenceau, which is never dull, day or night. By day there is the traffic of small shops, by night a profusion of restaurants packed with contented tourists ruining their digestion on rich fish soup and too much cheap wine. It was our only experience of Corsica in a summer mood. We dined in a restaurant in the square off Rue Clemenceau, in front of the church of Ste-Marie. Although it was late October, the tables outside were all taken and the air was thick with French, German and Dutch and a number of good smells. Yes, we had the fish soup and too much cheap wine: an enjoyable evening and a restless night.

We drove north along an excellent road to l'Ile-Rousse, passing Algajola, once one of the Genoese fortified cities around the coast. It suffered in the late eighteenth century from the competition of the new port created by Paoli a few kilometres north and today is better known for its good beach than its citadel or its long history as a port. When Paoli built his new port of d'Isola Rossa, l'Ile-Rousse today, in 1758 there was nothing here except for the remains of a Roman town and a Genoese tower. The new port enjoyed a greater success than its founder and there is still a bustle of commercial activity around the harbour and in the narrow streets between the waterfront and the central square, la place Paoli. The port's freight traffic has been bolstered in recent years by attracting some ten per cent of the island's ferry passengers.

The town is built around the Place Paoli, a pleasant if featureless square with four martial palms standing guard over a small fountain topped by a bust of Pasquale Paoli. On the west side is the austere façade of the parish church and scattered around the other sides are cafés where the local boulevardiers sip their pastis and their vins blancs and wrangle over local politics. If you find the centre of the town too hot and dusty, it is pleasant to wander around the perimeter enjoying the views of the harbour and further out to sea. By luck, wandering aimlessly and slightly lost around the port we found l'Ile-Rousse railway station on the line that runs through the mountains from Bastia to here and down the coast to Calvi (there is another line to Ajaccio via Corte). The *Chemins de Fer Corse* still operate a regular service but looking at this small station you might not have thought so. It was immediately obvious that the station master and his family lived upstairs. The upper storey was a frenzy of swinging shutters, a colourful display of washing, the screams of a baby and, at one window or another, a small face or the flourish of a feather duster. The platform was tidy and deserted and the three entrances firmly shuttered. Even the metre-gauge lines looked slightly rusty. For the intending traveller it would not have been encouraging. I do assure you there is a regular service. I have a copy of the timetable and I did, just once, see a railcar with its trailer rumbling through the mountains. I have even resolved that one day I will return to Corsica just to ride the railway across the spectacular scenery, including numerous viaducts and tunnels.

We arrived at St-Florent right at the end of October and the month-long spell of Indian summer broke. It had remained hot and clear as we drove across the rugged landscape of the Désert des Agriates. It was not as bleak as the name suggests with the maquis softening the spread of rock and all along the road tall yellow spikes of flowers and in the distance an isolated mountain peak with the spreading outline of Japan's Mount Fuji. There are few dull stretches of road in Corsica and what sometimes looks unpromising on the map in reality is nearly always interesting if not beautiful.

Apart from enjoying the view, as we approached St-Florent we searched our guide-books for a hotel. We liked the look of one on the coast a kilometre or two north of the town but as we drove through the centre we should have been warned by the air of desertion that hung over the place. After finding two hotels on the coast road closed for the winter we realised that here the season was over. Parking the car back in the main square, a grey sky, a sharpish wind and a few drops of rain confirmed the fact. We had been spoilt and the first taste of late autumn came as a shock.

The rain held off and we wandered around the deserted town. A few restaurants were still open but in the end we could find only one modern hotel on the main road which remained open all the year. It had no restaurant but the rooms were pleasant. Despite this chill welcome, I enjoyed St-Florent and, with its attractive harbour and its position facing onto the large bay, it must be most attractive in summer. Now, row upon row of small sailing boats were securely moored and battened down with canvas covers for the winter, their stays thrashing eerily against the metal masts in the wind. The old town, behind the restaurants on the quay, is small, without any real feature except the remains of the citadel and a picturesque charm.

If you follow the narrow lane running east from the war memorial in the centre of the town, in 1 km you will come to the site of the old Roman town of Nebbio. Here, as at Mariana, south of Bastia, the Pisans built one of their cathedrals in a place where the Christian tradition had flourished since later Roman times. Nothing remains of Roman Nebbio but it was the seat of a bishop by the fourth century and there must have been an early church here. Although many local Pisan churches survive throughout Corsica, La Canonica at Mariana and Santa-Maria-Assunta at Nebbio are the only two Pisan cathedrals in the island to survive. Fortunately, both are in good condition. La Canonica was consecrated in 1119 and clearly exercised an influence over the design of the Nebbio cathedral which is thought to have been finished about 1140. The overall design and the proportions of the two buildings are similar but there is a notable difference in the general style and the decoration. This may be explained partly by the difference of building materials. The soft, honey-coloured limestone at Nebbio immediately gives the cathedral a less austere and more sophisticated appearance. Undoubtedly, however, part of this sophistication must be due to the increasing skill of the Pisan craftsmen working in Corsica. There is a new elegance in the façade at Nebbio. The five tall blind arcades below are perfectly balanced by three similar but smaller arcades above, the skeleton of this design echoing the structure of the three naves in the interior. Carved stylised animals and geometrical patterns on the capitals relieve any monotony in the basic design of linked, repeating arches. Nebbio must represent the highest achievement of the Pisan masons working in Corsica. Here one can enjoy the perfect proportions of La Canonica set off by architectural detail which is as delicately balanced as the whole mass. It may be less austere but it has retained all the best qualities of simplicity.

It does give one a strange sensation to see this minor masterpiece of architecture seemingly stuck down in the midst of nowhere, like suddenly seeing a Chippendale commode standing in the middle of a field. Facing the entrance to the cathedral was a large, nineteenth-century family tomb, its classical columns gathering moss, the inscription obscured by the branches of the surrounding hedge. The cathedral was slightly raised above the road which ran along the south wall. The church does have an interesting interior and, in theory, the key can be obtained from the Syndicat d'Initiative in the centre of the town. Throughout Corsica smaller churches are usually kept locked. I have been reticent to write about the interiors of a number of churches knowing the difficulty of obtaining the key. In theory, there is always a key at some neighbouring house but even when you have identified the particular house it is far from certain that it will be occupied at that moment. The interior of the Nebbio cathedral is worth an effort but in many cases the frustration and time-wasting are poorly rewarded once the door is open.

We walked back along the lane, past another family memorial, alcoves on each side of the door containing statues of forlorn mourners, across the road a group of collapsing slum hovels and nearer the town the smell of freshly pressed grapes wafting down the road. The late afternoon had brightened and the main square of St-Florent had come to life with the attention of a large crowd centred on a game of boule. The game combines some of the skill of bowls with all the viciousness of the best croquet and I never cease to wonder how those bottle-nosed old Frenchmen can achieve such accuracy on such rough, pitted ground. The bombing shots are impressive but when the silver ball progresses by hops, skips and jumps amongst the gravel to roll within millimetres of the marker I am lost in admiration. It is certainly a game of character where style and personality combine in each measured movement. The game in progress was a perfect example. Like most games of boule it was being played with such seriousness, even ferocity, there was no way of telling whether one was the lucky spectator of the grand championship of Corsica or an off-the-cuff friendly match set up in the café opposite.

Of the four players, one of each pair seemed ordinary enough and on speaking terms with everybody. The other two were of different metal, an enormously tall man with a shock of wild hair and a stubbier character who shambled and muttered up and down the pitch. The tall man was a master of the bomb which crashed down onto his opponents' balls when they dared to come near the marker, scattering them among the legs of the spectators. The shambler specialised in devastatingly accurate ground work. His body trembled its way through a corkscrew movement, the thick wrist flicked upwards and a second later, amidst a shower of dust and pebbles every ball scattered away except his which was suddenly motionless, cheek to cheek with the marker. These two veterans played an ugly game, intimidating their opponents with personality and skill. Each throw of the ball was the strike of a cobra. Suddenly, the game was over and it was all smiles and friendly back-slapping as they retired to the café to wet their whistles or whatever it is that exhausted boule players do. Village cricket, pub darts – there is nothing on earth quite like boule.

17 The port and surrounding old town with new development, Ajaccio

18 Napoleon in the Place Maréchal-Foch, Ajaccio

19 View of the old town, Corte

20 The citadel crowning the old town, Corte

10

The Granite Crown

THE MOUNTAINS OF CORSICA

Since I first went to Corsica in 1963, many times people have asked me if I would recommend a holiday there. I have always urged them to go and invariably they have asked what I liked most about the island. My answer was, and remains, the marvellous variety of the mountainous landscape. In a small island such as Corsica, with so much natural beauty compressed into such a confined area, the view changes every few kilometres, particularly wherever you climb from the coast to the mountains. To illustrate my enthusiasm I always recalled one particular drive.

It was a spring morning of gold and blue. The sea lapped against the foundations of our hotel, rippling away in a trembling surface of aquamarine, the water sparkling in the sun. On the horizon the sky rose to enclose our world in a dome of the palest blue, untouched by a single cloud. A stone quay ran out from one side of the hotel. Built into it was a tank where lobsters for the table were kept sea-fresh in captivity. Those clumsy, blue crustaceans fumbled their way across the sandy bottom of the tank, the plates of their shells overlapping like Japanese armour.

I was an obsessive fisherman in those days and had come to Corsica with a bundle of rods and other equipment. After breakfast I stood on the quay and prepared my spinning rod for an hour of sea-fishing. The morning was so beautiful that it was difficult to concentrate on assembling my equipment. Fishing is often as much about enjoying one's surroundings as catching fish. At moments like this, even with the rod in one's hand, one half-forgets why one has come. It was one of those days.

Although at heart a dry-fly purist, that morning I enjoyed flicking the long line out across the water. I did not really expect to catch anything and my efforts were not even rewarded with a sardine. It was time to move on. I dismantled my rod with as much satisfaction as if I had had a creel full of sea trout at my feet. Now, in my obsessive state and with a remarkably patient wife, I was looking forward to finding a stretch of trout water in the mountains.

Leaving the sea and the white beach behind us, we began to climb into the mountains which rose immediately behind the fishing port. At first the road wound up among the rocks and groups of acacia, ilex and chestnut trees against the background of the maquis and stretches of rough grass. It was an open landscape full of sunshine and cool shade. Before we had climbed far I found my trout stream. We parked by a handsome but broken-backed stone Genoese bridge. Its half-arch cast a perfect shadow in the clear water. The river was shallow, bubbling its way between rocks and over beds of stones. It was hard to believe that trout could swim in this depth of water. But I soon had my rod together. This was wet-fly water and I was obliged to put away the snobberies of the dry-fly purist.

It was a perfect place: the silvered stream, banks of grass and wildflowers and everywhere the fresh brightness of spring with the nearest mountains rising above the trees into the silent sky. My fly was tossed by the water from pebble to pebble. I followed it, now bent double under a canopy of branches. The stream was running downwards through a coppice whose shade darkened the water. The stream seemed to have become even shallower. I could feel my line and my fly dragging on the stony bed. A low branch forced me onto my knees. The shade deepened and my line felt heavier.

'Better reel in,' I thought. 'I'm not going to catch anything here, no water.' My thumb and forefinger closed on the small handle of the reel. I began to reel in and – *snap*; the unmistakable feel of a fish on the line.

It is always the moment of truth. This particular moment seemed more truthful than most. 'Heavens!' I thought, my hands trembling with the surprise. 'It can't be. There's no water.' I applied tentative pressure to the reel and there was that familar resistance, not a dead weight but an equalising living pressure at the other end. Then, coming out of my state of shock, I saw it, a straining flash of silver across the stream. In common parlance, I had a bite.

Life is full of pleasant anticlimaxes. It took me all of fifteen seconds to land the trout. It weighed slightly under half a pound. It was certainly no leviathan but catching that small Corsican trout gave me a thrill – and a surprise – that have lasted for twenty-five years. That night at our mountain inn they cooked the trout for our supper. The kitchen showed their disdain by serving the fish on the largest dish in the establishment. I accepted this sneer. At least my trout had been caught fairly with a wet-fly. I knew well that the locals prefer to fish with salmon eggs or dynamite, probably after dark. The penalties are draconian.

We drove on, the road becoming steeper and climbing through a series of sharp bends. Already we had left two different landscapes behind; the glare of the beach and the sea, and the sun and green shade of woods and the river. Now we were ascending into another, more sombre world where the mountains came closer, at places towering immediately above the road. We were now in a forest of great pines and the shade was darker and chillier. But everywhere along the verges of the road were tall clumps of hellebore. They were spectacular but their vivid green in the gloomy shade of the pines was slightly sinister. The small, creamy flowers hung in a delicate innocence but there was something venomous about the stems and foliage, a suggestion of strange snakes poised amongst the crusted trunks of the pines.

Where the mountainside fell away from the road to the valley below there were frequent glimpses between the trees of the view over the roof of the forest. The upper branches of the trees formed an intricate pattern which spread across the floor of the valley and up to meet the line of mountains which filled the distance. In the deep shade of the forest the pine branches were almost black. Where they spread across the valley the sun wove into this carpet many shades of green, like another kind of sea below the cliffs of granite piling up against the skyline opposite. The great pine forest was impressive, silent and menacing.

As we neared the pass, the landscape petrified into bleak

tundra. It was cold. Mist obscured the immediate view and wet cloud drifted around the crags that now walled us in. Scree and broken rock were scattered around the foot of the cliffs and a few dead pines stood grotesque as scarecrows, stripped white by the wind. It was an empty barren world, a thousand kilometres from bright beaches and dappled shade. In reality, it was little more than 1200 m and 40 winding km from both. The compression of so much mountainous country into such a small area is what gives the Corsican landscape such sudden and distinctive variety.

I can still remember each detail of that drive and I must have described it to many people over the years. A few friends may have gone to Corsica on the strength of it and I once included it in a travel article for *Country Life*. For twenty-five years it remained in my mind as the drive which best illustrated the variety of the Corsican scene and the extraordinary contrasts one encountered in 40 or 50 km. We made many drives in 1963 but that was the one I enjoyed and remembered best.

I must now confess that when I toured the island again in 1986, I could not find that route. Although each detail did exist, somehow I had built up a composite journey in my mind. I think that the basic route must have been the spectacular drive from Porto up through Evisa to the forest of Aitone and the heights of the Col de Vergio. The outlines of the landscape are all there and memory has embellished them with lobster-tanks and broken Genoese bridges borrowed from other occasions. My confusion may have been increased by the fact that in 1963 I set out along that road from Porto and in 1986 I drove along it in the opposite direction. These spectacular mountain roads ideally should be enjoyed from both directions since the views often appear almost entirely different. Doubling back on your tracks may waste time but it is seldom monotonous.

Apart from a stretch of the east coast road, in Corsica you are always near the mountains and usually driving amongst them. Although the highest mountain, Monte Cinto, is only 2710 m and many of the island's mountains are below 2000 m, their density in such a small area and their dramatic granite formations give the mountain landscape a grandeur far beyond its actual size. In spring, when there is still snow on the higher peaks and ranges but warmth in the valleys and along the coast, Corsica is an alpine paradise. You will see no snow in October but I do think there is a mellowness in the autumn sunshine that brings out the extraordinary range of colours in the Corsican granite, by the sea or in the mountains.

Geologically, Corsica is a great fist of granite thrusting up out of the Mediterranean with its northern area of schist and patches of porphyry and limestone. So homogeneous and so small, you would be entitled to think that the island's landscape, though surprisingly grandiose, was likely to be monotonous; a series of similar mountains and gorges; one pine forest like another and the small valleys all alike with their chestnut trees clustered amongst the maquis. The ultimate wonder of Corsica is its infinite variety and the way in which comparatively few natural elements manage to combine to produce an ever-changing scene.

There are four gorges running westward from the neighbourhood of Corte: Restonica, Tavignano, the Scala di Santa Regina and Asco. The entrances to all four are separated only by 26 km and the gorges, Monte Cinto and other high mountains between them are contained in an area roughly 28 by 22 km. They are built of the same granite, in many places sharing views of the same mountains, mountains rising from the same maquis and similar pine forests. Yet each gorge has its own beauty, its own drama and a distinctive character. The mountains are so massed and shaped that a slight difference of angle or altitude can change a peak or range beyond recognition. In many places in these gorges the cliff faces are barren and precipitous but none of them rivals the drama of the Scala di Santa Regina, one of the most menacing landscapes in Corsica.

There is one other element which can bring dramatic changes to the mountain landscape and which some, mistakenly I think, will find less welcome. Throughout this book I have rhapsodized about the perfect weather, spring and autumn. That is mostly true but when you drive up into the higher mountains from the bright coast, you must always be prepared for darkening skies and sudden storms. That is the way of mountains everywhere and the mountains of Corsica are high enough to wrap themselves in cloud and rain while below the woods and the beaches enjoy a perfect day. It is not inevitable but if you tour the whole of Corsica without a single mountain storm, in a limited sense you will be lucky. You will also have missed the most dramatic view of these harsh mountains when they reveal themselves in angry mood and show a side of the Corsican landscape which must have made its contribution to the implacable Corsican character. Without any malice, I hope you have one fierce mountain storm along your way and that you are philosophical enough to put away your camera and record the spectacle in your memory.

Needless to say, we had our storm in October on the mountain drive to which I had most looked forward. The route northwards from Porto-Vecchio through the mountains to Ghisoni is one of the most spectacular drives in Corsica and, on a fine day, most photogenic. As we drove across the narrow coastal plain from Porto-Vecchio the bright morning promised well. By the time we had climbed into the deep shade of the Forêt de l'Ospédale, the view back to the coast still glinted with sunlight but around us the weather was already grumbling and the water of the lake on our left was dull and reflecting gathering clouds. The blackening sky darkened the shade of the forests and each pass became more obscured by the wet mist thickening in the rain.

I had particularly looked forward to seeing the small town of Ghisoni again. It lies in a deep valley, enclosed by the forests of Marmano and Sorba and dominated to the south-east by the scarred, rocky escarpments of Christe Eleison and Kyrie Eleison, transcendental names borrowed from the liturgy of the Holy Mass. On that day, when we looked across this celebrated view, there was a different awesome presence; the great rocks were veiled in swirling rain clouds, the valley was a cauldron of mist, steel lines of rain cut into the trees and thunder ran through the surrounding mountains. Ghisoni was almost invisible. This was a landscape of mist, rain and cloud but in that setting spectacular and memorable.

Our long drive that day had a comic climax which showed that even the foothills of Corsica hold surprises. The road from

Ghisoni leads you back easily enough onto the excellent main road (N 193) running down the mountains to Ajaccio. We planned to follow this road, itself offering fine views, to the small side road leading to Bastelica – the birthplace of Sampiero Corso – a village, we had heard, where Corsican charcuterie and cheese were still made by hand. We passed through the village of Bocognano and almost immediately we saw our turning sign-posted to the left, the D 27 to Bastelica. We were now following the smallest of white roads on the Michelin map which we thought we had read with great care.

It was a pretty road, leading through orchards, meadows and the occasional group of humble farm buildings. By one gate were a flock of sheep and a sight I had not seen throughout our 1986 tour: a genuine rural character. There, amidst his sheep and perched most precariously on a donkey, was a Corsican shepherd, battered hat, broad black cummerbund and a disintegrating umbrella stuck under his saddle-bags and miscellaneous packages. In that fleeting glimpse he seemed as exotic as a Victorian chimney-sweep or the faded photographs in Bastia's folk museum.

The road wound on another few kilometres, crossed a bridge and a metre or two beyond disappeared into the brambles which grew in a well-established thicket across the road. The D 27 appeared to have expired. I got out and struggled through the brambles to discover that the road, largely crumbled, continued on the other side and in bits and pieces wandered around the next bend and up the hill. There was no hope of progress and turning back I noticed that just after the brambles several metres of the road had at some time slipped down the hill in a small landslide. This was not the way to Bastelica.

It was puzzling. Roads marked on a Michelin map do not normally peter out in the undergrowth. Michelin maps match British Admiralty charts for accuracy, sandbanks or landslides. We looked again at the map, peering more carefully at the web of white roads. Of course, we, not Michelin, were at fault. With infallible accuracy this road was shown as coming to an abrupt end almost immediately after crossing the bridge. It was deceptive since the road came to life again nearer Bastelica and gave the appearance of going all the way to the village. We were forced to return to the main road and take the D 127 a short way on, passing through Tavera. This was an exceptionally steep and winding road which, from where it turned back into the D 27, had the worst surface we experienced in Corsica. My car was already in poor shape with an exhaust pipe likely to part company with us at any moment. The deep pot-holes and corrugated ruts produced noises suggesting that the engine might drop off. I don't suppose it was more than 12 km but they were the longest in Corsica. The next day, wandering around Bastelica, we found a notice where the road left the centre of the village advising drivers to avoid it. They might have put up a similar notice at the other end. No doubt the locals are familiar with the hazards of these short cuts and drive to Bastelica the long way round on the major road. Elsewhere, although the white roads were often narrow, the surface was always reasonable.

By the time we reached Bastelica it was dusk and we were tired. When Yuki told me that we had driven only just over 200 km I could hardly believe her. That day we seemed to have driven through several worlds and several climates. Even as we stretched our legs before dinner, strolling up the hill beyond the hotel, the heavy grunt of pigs in their hovels just above the road and the lights of the village twinkling up through the branches of the chestnuts and the apple trees composed a further landscape for our pleasure.

The hotel was comfortable, the dinner excellent and the following morning we had breakfast on a small terrace looking down onto Bastelica cradled in orchards and woodland. I have to admit that usually distance does lend enchantment to the view of these Corsican villages, whether you see them from above or below. When we descended into the centre of Bastelica its charm evaporated leaving us with a plain church, an unheroic statue of Sampiero Corso which made the national hero look like an overacting chorus member in *Il Trovatore* and not much else. The streets were empty and the single café opposite the church looked unwelcoming. We failed to find anyone making the famous

Corsican goats' and ewes' milk cheese. As for the homemade charcuterie, we did eventually find a modern factory below the village. It looked an efficient cooperative whose sausage-making machinery would not start up until mid-winter. No doubt, the Bastelican workers clocked-in just like their sisters in the factories of Birmingham and Baltimore. It was disappointing but we were glad we had come. Handmade or machine-made, the charcuterie at dinner the previous evening had been delicious. We tourists do tend to linger in the past.

I shall return to Corsica. When I look back on my two journeys around the island I am grateful for everything we saw but aware of much we missed. I regret that I never made the journey by train across the mountains from Bastia down to l'Ile-Rousse. It must offer many spectacular views as it winds high above the road. The most intimate view of Corsica can only be available to those who have the time, energy and enterprise to walk the 220-km marked trail right across the Parc Natural Régional, called the sentier de Grande Ranndonnée (GR 20). It takes two weeks, walking five to eight hours each day, and runs diagonally through the heart of the mountains from near Calvi in the north to near Porto-Vecchio in the south. The trail is recommended between mid-July to the end of October but walkers must be fit and properly equipped.

Despite these exhortations, most people will see Corsica from their car or bus and it is one of the virtues of the island that the roads lead you so quickly and easily into the heart of the mountains. I have now driven along most of the famous routes and stood admiringly at the top of nearly all the most spectacular passes. I have enjoyed Corsica in spring and autumn and found it so full of variety that I know that I could never tire of its landscapes. There is an obvious beauty in the maquis, the wild flowers, the great forests, the magnificent coast and the changing seasons. But similar attractions exist in many other places and they do not account for the unique quality of the Corsican landscape. It is the granite rock that is the heart of the island's grandeur, austere but splendid. It seems a dense, intractable and monotonous material but in Corsica it is the mirror to the sun. It catches each change of light and the crystals of its surface transmute it into a miraculous spectrum of colours.

I have struggled to capture this interplay of sun and rock in words. Often the colours have a subtlety which defeats photography and would challenge the skilled painter. Only at that moment when you stand looking over the sharp escarpment of the flamingo-pink Calanche and out across the quiet blue water of the Golfe de Porto to the burning orange rock of La Scandola, will you know for yourself why you came to Corsica.

Some Practical Information

Introduction

The information in these notes is primarily intended for individual travellers who wish to explore the whole or part of Corsica rather than to visit the island for a summer beach-holiday. However, I have started by giving some information which I hope will be helpful to the summer visitor in planning a holiday in Corsica. After that I have concentrated on information for the individual traveller and, particularly, the motorist. However, some of this information will be useful to anyone visiting Corsica. It is a small island and in all the larger summer resorts there are bus excursions to the main places of interest so that summer visitors are not confined to their particular beach but have an opportunity to enjoy a wider view of the island. These notes do not pretend to be a definitive guide, particularly in the recommendation of resorts, hotels or restaurants. The French Government Tourist Office (178 Piccadilly, London W1V 0AL; 01-491 7622) and any good travel agent can supply you with detailed information. I have avoided giving times, prices and any other information which goes out of date. My main intention in compiling these notes has been to share useful practical experiences with the reader, information not always found in the official guide-books.

Visas

When increasing terrorism broke out in Paris in the summer of 1986, the French government introduced regulations requiring nearly everyone except nationals of EEC countries to obtain a visa before entering France which, of course, includes Corsica. If you are going to Corsica check with your travel agent if you will require a visa, which is valid for three months and can be renewed for a further three months at any French consulate. You could also obtain this information from the French Government Tourist Office or your nearest French consulate. If you do require a visa you will need a valid passport, one passport photograph and a good deal of patience.

SUMMER HOLIDAY INFORMATION

When to go

If you wish to spend all or most of your time in Corsica enjoying a beach-holiday, the best season is from late June to mid-September. It is also the most crowded. By the middle of September, though, the weather may still be beautiful, the temperature of the sea drops and the days begin to shorten. That is also the end of the recognised season and the beach-holiday facilities – including some hotels and camp sites – will start to close. I saw a small number of late seaside holidaymakers in October but I noticed the the majority were not swimming.

How to go

If you want to go to Corsica in the high summer season, *book early*. Flights and car ferries are heavily booked and if you want to take a car you should have your ferry booked by the end of the previous February. The car ferries are good value compared to the English Channel fares but taking a car, or car and caravan from northern Europe is expensive and time-consuming. More detailed information about the ferries is given in the *Individual Travel* section. For a beach holiday a package tour will offer the best value. There are package tours from all over Europe to every beach resort in Corsica. These tours will include transport, usually a direct flight to the Corsican airport nearest to your resort. If you are tempted to take you own car so that you can enjoy the beach and also explore the island, I must warn you that during July and August you will find it almost impossible to get a hotel room near the coast and difficult inland where there are few hotels anyway. July and August are not months for touring in Corsica. At that time you will be wiser to choose a sympathetic base and leave the touring to the one-day bus excursions.

Where to go

Corsica offers a basic choice for the beach-holiday. You can go either to one of the resorts based on a town or to a hotel or camping site in a more remote area where the main attractions are the beach and the sea. I have to admit that I have never been to Corsica in high summer so any suggestions I make about summer resorts are based on observations made in spring and autumn. You start from two basic assumptions. Corsica in July and August will be hot and, in most places, crowded. But that is now true of all popular Mediterranean resorts.

I would avoid Ajaccio and Bastia. They may have the bright lights but they also have a lot of traffic, noise and a daily struggle to a beach. Of the smaller towns I like Calvi. It has a fine beach and excellent tourist facilities yet it has remained unspoilt. Porto-Vecchio offers similar attractions but is smaller and more congested than Calvi. Two attractive fishing villages are Porto and Centuri. Porto is livelier and has a superb coast and inland scenery. Centuri would be ideal for anyone wishing to get away from it all. For beach resorts away from towns I liked the north coast of the Gulf of Valinco, opposite Propriano. There are a number of new resorts south of Bastia along the east coast.

In Corsica, as in all of France, one of the pleasures of the holiday is trying different restaurants. If you are going to stay in or near a town, try to find accommodation that offers a demi-pension and allows you to eat out once a day. I did stay in two package-tour hotels in 1986 and the pension menu was dull compared to the hotels' table-d'hôte menus. There are a large number of hotels in Corsica which do not have a restaurant and serve only breakfast. This would leave you free to have a picnic lunch and to dine out in the evening. Most restaurants offer at least two menus, many three, at different prices. The house wine is usually the best value.

When you choose a hotel from a brochure ask for detailed

information not least about its exact location. I was walking up the main street of Porto when I passed one of its largest hotels. By the entrance was displayed a copy of their brochure. Alluring photographs showed a typical double-bedroom and a view of the dining room. By ingenious photography both rooms appeared to look immediately over the sea. In reality the hotel was 100 m from the sea with a noisy road and a car park in between. And in Corsica the more expensive hotels do not always occupy the best positions or offer the best value. Porto is a good example. Both times I have been there I stayed in what may well have been Porto's first and only hotel and for that reason it has a charming position hanging right over the port and the sea. It was still extremely simple but had all the comfort one requires in hot weather and an excellent terrace restaurant into the bargain. The more expensive hotels in Porto are the new ones which had little choice in finding sites and which are devoid of any atmosphere. I dined at one and spent and whole meal fighting off the owner's menagerie of underfed cats and dogs.

Corsica now has dozens of resorts. This brief note can do no more than give a slight idea of the Corsican summer scene. If you want a good beach-holiday, research thoroughly and book early. The following notes for the individual traveller, though more concerned with the pleasures and problems of touring the whole island, may be of some help to you in planning your summer holiday along with the main text of the book.

INDIVIDUAL TRAVELLERS: EXPLORING THE ISLAND

When to go

The two seasons for exploring the island are from late April to the end of May and late September to late October. At these times you are likely to have good weather and no difficulty anywhere in finding accommodation. If it is possible, go in May when the maquis is flowering and the island is most beautiful. The spring weather is perfect for sightseeing though it will not be warm enough to swim. The autumn is a golden season when it is likely to be as hot as a good English summer. The countryside remains green and it is possible to swim if you are hardy. Towards the end of October the days start to get shorter. Spring or autumn, nobody can promise you fine weather every day. But I do not think you will have enjoyed the full magic of the Corsican landscape unless you have driven over one of the high passes with the surrounding mountains shrouded in rain and cloud, the surrounding forest dark and the sky angry. A storm brings out the lurking malevolence in the granite landscape of Corsica.

How to go

There are three ways of travelling around Corsica. You can take your own transport, hire a car on arrival or, if you have plenty of time, use the limited local transport.

For those who wish to take their own car or motorbike there is an excellent and reasonable ferry service between mainland France and several Corsican ports run by the Société Nationale Maritime Corse-Méditerranée (SNCM). Their London office is 178 Piccadilly, W1, next door to the French Government Tourist Office. They issue an excellent information booklet, *Guide du Passager*, and seasonal timetables. It is most convenient to go overnight, the longest route a journey of ten hours. There is a wide choice of 1st and 2nd class cabins, the cheapest of which are clean and comfortable. At the time of writing the choice of routes is as follows:

> Marseilles to Ajaccio/Bastia/l'Ile-Rousse/Propriano.
> Nice to Ajaccio/Bastia/Calvi/l'Ile-Rousse/Propriano.
> Toulon to Ajaccio/Bastia/Calvi/l'Ile-Rousse/Propriano.

Marseilles to Bastia and Propriano both take ten hours and Nice to Calvi only five hours. I must repeat that if you consider using these car ferries in July, August and early September, make your booking before the end of February. When embarking, you are required to be at the quay one hour before departure. All the boats have restaurants or cafeterias or both. The frequency of sailings varies according to the season and there are not daily sailings from each port. It is essential to obtain a copy of the SNCM timetable. Out of season it is normally easy to change your port of departure and fares are identical between Marseilles and Ajaccio and Bastia for example. I cannot predict future prices but it may give you some idea of what to expect if I compare the autumn 1986 price for two people and a small car of £110 Dover to Calais return with Marseilles to Bastia return, including 2nd class couchettes for two, at £164. Loading and unloading of cars is quick and simple.

Some people may think it quicker and more convenient to explore Corsica with a fly/drive holiday. Much of the seeming extra cost may be offset by your saving on car ferries, the cost of driving through France and insurance. There is the further advantage that if anything goes wrong with your hire car, even on the remotest mountain road, someone else is responsible for recovering the car and providing you with another. I know from personal experience that a breakdown with one's own car in Corsica can be time-wasting and expensive. Spare parts for non-French cars are usually only obtainable in Ajaccio and Bastia.

Bicycles and motorbikes can be taken on the ferries besides individuals with no vehicle. I saw many people touring Corsica on a motorbike and a few cycles. To cycle around Corsica I think you would need the maximum number of gears and a high standard of fitness since for a great deal of the time you would be pedalling up punishing hills and mountains.

There is public transport in Corsica for those without their own vehicle. I will deal with it in a separate section.

Insurance

Whether you take your own vehicle or hire one in Corsica, I would advise you to take out the maximum insurance cover. If you take your own car you should obtain a *green card* from your insurance company. The additional cover it gives you is worth the additional cost. I do not wish to exaggerate the hazards of Corsica's roads. It is a case of better safe than sorry.

21 Double bay protected by old Genoese watchtower, Porto

22 A diminished fishing fleet, Porto

23 Statuary on a roadside tomb, St-Florent

24 Pigs scavenging for chestnuts

Sardinia

Sardinia is only 19 km south of Corsica with regular car ferries from Bonifacio. There is also a direct French car ferry from Toulon to Porto Torres in northern Sardinia. It makes an interesting holiday to visit both islands, not least because they are so different. I would strongly advise you to visit Sardinia before Corsica. Corsica is more interesting and beautiful and although Sardinia is worth visiting, it might prove an anticlimax after Corsica.

Motoring

It is easiest to explore Corsica and to appreciate the varied character of the island with a car or motorbike. The majority of the island's roads are exceptionally narrow and precipitous, falling away into the sea or deep valleys. These corniche and mountain roads open up magnificent landscapes but demand exceptional care and concentration which often prevent the driver from enjoying the scenery without stopping the car. Touring Corsica by car is pleasanter if there are two drivers.

Apart from the normal hazards of blind corners, the local drivers tend to take them too fast and in the middle of the road. One might argue that the locals know the roads and what they are doing. The large number of gashed and dented Corsican cars and the wrecks at the roadside contradict that argument. There is a lot of aggressive driving and few locals use their horns on blind corners. You just have to drive slowly on these roads. I gave up alcohol for lunch as it blurred my concentration. I do not wish to exaggerate the dangers of Corsican roads but they do require a clear head.

Maps and map reading

Only one map is essential for motoring in Corsica. This is the excellent Michelin map of Corsica, Sheet 90 in their set of maps covering France. The scale is 1 cm to 2 km. It is an infallible road map and through various symbols and coding it gives a a lot of useful tourist information. Although it is a large-scale map, it can become a test for one's eyesight where the most minor roads twist through the mountains. I failed the test and next time I shall take a map-reading magnifying glass. If you do lose your way, blame yourself, not your Michelin map.

The majority of the roads in Corsica have good to reasonable surfaces. A few of the minor roads are terrible and have to be taken slowly. The signposting and road numbering is far behind mainland France. To make matters worse an enormous number of the island's signposts have been made illegible by daubed political slogans and, quite often, by bullet holes. The lack of the normal French kilometre stone giving the road number was a great inconvenience and in some of the remoter areas frequent reference to the map was essential.

Distances and timing

Corsica is a small island, 183 km long and 83 km wide; hardly more than 100 by 50 miles. For the motorist these distances are most deceptive. In 1986 when we visited most of the beautiful and interesting places in the island, without retracing our steps we drove just over 2400 km or 1500 miles. Many days on the slow coast or mountain roads I drove for seven or eight hours averaging only 40 kph or 25 mph. When planning a route in Corsica you would be wise to calculate in terms of covering 25 miles an hour. That reckoning will give you ample time for stops at viewing points, for photography and to enjoy what you have come to see without hurrying. It does not include a lunch stop.

Petrol

The situation is much better than it used to be. However, when you set out for a long drive in the remoter parts of the island it is wise to leave with a full tank. Apart from anything else, in small mountain towns garages close for a long lunch break and if you want petrol just after they have closed, you may have to wait two hours for it.

Garages and repairs

Ajaccio and Bastia have garages representing every well-known make of car, European and Japanese. My Volkswagen had a new tyre in Bastia and a new exhaust pipe in Ajaccio. The work was carried out efficiently and at a reasonable cost. The garages in the small towns looked efficient but might take time to get spare parts. Once I had a puncture on a remote road. The first car to come along stopped and the driver asked if I needed help. I felt that you would not be left stranded in Corsica; the remoteness of these roads encourages a certain camaraderie.

Winter motoring

Should you be motoring in Corsica during the winter, although the coast may be mild, remember that there will be snow on the high passes. Conditions at these points are well signposted.

Public transport

With patience and perseverance it is still possible to travel in Corsica by public transport. But unless you have a great deal of time, you would be wise to concentrate on those areas covered by better services. There are local buses. Some link the main towns and some cover more rural routes. I did not often see them on the roads but they exist and the French Government Tourist Office could supply more detailed information.

Of more interest is the metre-gauge railway which was first constructed around 1897 and which in itself offers an intriguing 'magic carpet' holiday to the northern half of Corsica. The railway, modernised in 1983, runs through mountainous areas where no car or bus can follow. It offers 232 km of superb views; zigzagging, soaring, plunging from Bastia to Corte and to Ajaccio, twisting and turning through Ponte Leccio down to l'Ile-Rousse and Calvi. Every visitor to Corsica ought to take at least one mountain ride on this unique line. The mountain routes offer marvellous views for photographers and, for once, the motorist can give his or her whole attention to the landscape. For the railway buff it must rank high amongst the mountain railways of Europe (see *Railway Magazine*, Dec. 1986). A timetable can be obtained from the French Government Tourist Office and the railway offers the perfect transport for a holiday in Corsica. It hardly needs a puff from me. The line is now carrying about half a million passengers each year.

Climbing and walking

There are superb opportunities for climbing and walking in Corsica all of which are clearly described in an excellent book, *Corsica Mountains*, started by Eric Roberts before his death on Annapurna and finished by Robin Collomb. The book is full of practical information for the mountain walker and scrambler. Full descriptions of routes are given up to Grade III with briefer references to more difficult routes. The central mountain region of Corsica is now protected within the area that the French government have designated the Parc Naturel Régional (PNR). The area is unspoilt but also has few facilities for the walker or climber. Anyone considering even the simplest hike in this area ought to begin by reading Roberts and Collomb.

Corsican food

Corsica has an individual tradition of cooking. Over the centuries local ingredients have been prepared under Italian and French influences. Genuine Corsican cooking has always belonged in the home rather than in the restaurant and that is now truer than ever. Restaurant menus offer a limited number of Corsican specialities but they do not show the range of domestic cooking, perhaps because the average visitor would not like many traditional dishes of simple ingredients pungently flavoured with herbs from the maquis.

There are a limited number of Corsican specialities which you will find in restaurants and several of which you can buy in shops in all the larger towns. Although these products are local, they are not cheap. Corsicans pride themselves on their smoked hams and pork charcuterie. There is the smoked ham called *prisutto* which I find a leathery cousin to the delicate Italian *prosciutto*. Smoked and spiced charcuterie include *lonzu, coppa* and the *salciccie* sausages from the Niolo and La Rocca areas. They are all interesting but they are hard and dry compared to their French equivalents. They are what they are, peasant food. But that is no reason not to try them even if they are no longer offered at peasant prices.

Soups and stews are the cornerstone of domestic cooking but with the exception of fish soup I seldom saw them on any menu. In one simple hotel in the mountains we did have a diluted *minestra*, a vegetable soup which included red beans. And at Corte I had a magnificent stew of wild boar. I would not have believed that it was possible to make a game flesh so tender. We did find one other delicacy in Corte. We were searching for a picnic before setting out for a day in the mountains. In a bread shop just by the Place Paoli we found some long, thin pasties. They were made of a light pastry and filled with a liquid delicately flavoured with herbs of the maquis. They were very good and later we found three shops around the square selling them.

Corsica is famous for its fish, lobsters, a wide selection of Mediterranean fish on the coast, trout in the mountains. A Corsican version of bouillabaisse is found all around the coast and so is an excellent but less expensive fish soup, usually a meal in itself. Varieties of fish soup are found all round the Mediterranean but I thought the Corsican version particularly good. An enormous bowl of soup is served accompanied by toasted or baked slices of baguette which are floated in the soup as giant croutons after they have been lavishly smeared with mayonnaise laced with chilli pepper and the bottom of the toast rubbed with a clove of raw garlic. Cheese is sprinkled on the top and as I gaze at it I know the penalties that will follow. It is extremely rich.

Corsica is famous for its cheeses made from the milk of goats and ewes. Much of this milk is now exported to mainland France for the production of Roquefort cheese. Although I like these types of cheese, again I prefer those made in mainland France. For my taste the Corsican cheeses have a coarse flavour which makes them too strong. Cheese is used in Corsican cooking, particularly in a form called *brocciu* in which ewes' cheese is beaten with milk and heated, the resultant liquid used as an ingredient in a variety of dishes. In restaurants it is often offered as a filling for omelettes.

Chestnut flour was for a long time part of the Corsican staple diet but to my disappointment I found it used only in a flat, sweet cake based on a chestnut leaf. They are pleasant and can be found all over Corsica. Where the flour is still produced I never found out. We were told of a remote mountain village where the local wives still made traditional charcuterie. After an agonising drive over what must have been the most pot-holed road in Corsica we reached the village. I cannot deny that we had been told a *version* of the truth. The local wives did make charcuterie. They all clocked-in to a small modern factory at eight-thirty each morning.

I must end this section by adding that quite apart from Corsican specialities, during our 1986 tour of the island we had only one poor meal. Some meals were simpler than others. Occasionally, the service was so bad that it spoilt the meal but the food was always interesting and appetising. More often it was excellent simple French food matched by excellent local wines. I should add that we always ate at modest restaurants and there must be some expensive restaurants in Corsica which offer *haute cuisine* although there are few which earn a Michelin *rosette*.

Corsican wines and other drinks

The wines of Corsica have much improved in quality during the last quarter-century. It is not a place for great wines but all over the island you will find wines which are exceptionally pleasant and reasonable. The variety of local wines now made in Corsica add an additional pleasure to a tour of the island.

The area around Patrimonio has long had the reputation for producing the best wines in Corsica. With improvements in other districts I doubt if the Patrimonio wines are now as superior as they used to be. The district produces excellent, full-bodied red wine, rosé and white. Cap Corse is also well known for its pleasant white wines. Good red wines are produced around Ajaccio and Sartène. Red, white and rosé wines are also made in the south of Corsica, on the east coast between Bastia and Solenzara and in the Balagne district around Calvi. But apart from these well-known districts, wine seems to be grown in most places except the mountains. Often the vineyards are not visible from the main road but in October your car will suddenly be filled with the heady smell of the first pressing.

Most restaurants offer a fair selection of Corsican wines. The famous names like Patrimonio are usually quite expensive. I like wine but I am not an expert. I enjoyed the wines of Corsica and would make a few suggestions based on my experience. It is interesting from time to time to buy a bottle of one of the famous wines but usually comparison with the cheaper wines did not justify the high price. Most of the best wines we drunk, both in terms of quality and value, were the 'house wines' of the restaurants. Generally speaking, the reds were best with lots of pleasant rosés but, apart from Cap Corse, the whites were harsh. It was perhaps significant that a number of wine lists had no Corsican white wines.

The advantage of the 'house wines' was they were always local wines and obviously the owner of the restaurant knew where to get the best value. I noticed several times in restaurants crowded with local people that the majority were drinking the 'house wine' and on those occasions it always proved to be particularly good. These wines may be specially bottled and labelled for the restaurant or served in a pottery pitcher. We had few disappointments.

In all the well-known wine-growing districts there are *caves* selling their wine and offering free tastings. It is interesting to make at least one visit but do not expect bargains. I did not think their prices were less than the shops. The trouble with tasting in a *cave* is that it is embarrassing to leave without buying any wine if you find you do not like it. I noticed that local people arrive at the *cave* with their own large plastic container and buy much cheaper wine pumped out of barrels. That is probably the best bargain and even the best wine. Or if you find a bottled 'house wine' in a restaurant that you particularly like, it is always worth asking the *patron* if he will sell you a few bottles. That way, you get your tasting without embarrassment and the advantage of his expert knowledge of the local wines.

Corsica produces a number of aperitifs and liqueurs. The island's pastis, the aniseed-based aperitif so popular in southern France, is admired by connoisseurs. There are two local liqueurs made of flavoured eau-de-vie. One is cédratine with a flavouring of the island's citrus fruit, the other a liqueur of the maquis, flavoured with arbutus, myrtle and mint. These local liqueurs are much the same price as the well-known liqueurs of the mainland.

Hotels

You will find a comprehensive list of hotels in the *Corsica Guide Bleu* and a selective list of recommended hotels in the *Michelin Rouge*. Hotels in France are officially graded – one star, two stars, etc – and these gradings are given in the *Guide Bleu*. Michelin have their own more definitive system. You will not find Michelin-recommended hotels everywhere in Corsica but wherever there is one you will find that place underlined in red on the Michelin map of Corsica, Sheet 90. I found the Michelin recommendations in Corsica, as always, most reliable.

I am not able to give a comprehensive list of Corsican hotels. In the itinerary I suggest in the next section I have given a brief description of each hotel which we stayed at during our 1986 tour of Corsica. Most were adequate, several excellent. Only the individual reader can judge if these hotels will be to their taste. But the list will give you an idea of the quality and range of cheaper hotels in Corsica. Please remember that in many of the remoter parts of Corsica there are only simple hotels.

The typical one-star hotel in Corsica has rooms with tiled floors, a shower but no lavatory in the room, a bedside light hardly as effective as a candle and a bed that is no aid to a bad back. But they are clean, good value and frequently have an excellent restaurant. The two-star hotels have better-equipped and decorated rooms and bathrooms but the restaurants were seldom better and the bedside lighting could be even worse. Some of the hotels we stayed in were austere, none was bad.

In spring and autumn, the seasons which I have recommended for touring the island, you should have no difficulty in finding a hotel room anywhere, provided that the hotel is open. At many seaside resorts there are hotels which cater only for the summer season and which close early in October and in the interior there are a few hotels which close for the winter. This is not a serious problem but when your destination has only one small hotel, it is wise to arrive and book in not later than 5 p.m. On more than one occasion we arrived about then to find an empty hotel but by dinner time it was full. The *Guide Bleu*'s comprehensive list of hotels not only indicates those which are not open the whole year but also gives telephone numbers. If in any doubt it is wise to telephone to book in advance. The hotels in the small mountain towns are not primarily for tourists but for Corsicans travelling on business and they use these hotels all the year round.

On a few occasions we stayed in hotels which had no restaurant. In every case they served an excellent breakfast and recommended one or more good and reasonable local restaurants.

Restaurants

In Ajaccio and Bastia and all the main coastal resorts there is a wide choice of restaurants, varying in price and most of them offering two to three different menus from the economic tourist menu to the expensive gastronomic feast which usually includes the local specialities. In the larger mountain towns such as Corte and Sartène there are also a number of restaurants but in the smaller inland towns and villages the only restaurant may be the one in your hotel. All restaurants, following the French fashion, display their menus outside the establishment. Where there is a choice of restaurants it always pays to wander around the town comparing menus and deciding which restaurant you think looks most attractive. There are some expensive restaurants in Corsica but most of the restaurants are on the same price level and most offer good value. Their prices are roughly equivalent to mainland France but the service and, sometimes, the food is of a slightly lower general standard.

Wherever tourists go in numbers you will find cheap eating places serving crêpes, pizzas and hamburgers and other fast foods. Many bakers and patisseries sell hot pies and slices of pizza. Some of the cheap eating places may be closed out of season but I noticed in several places that they are becoming popular with young Corsicans.

Cafés

There are cafés throughout the island. The Corsicans like to keep to themselves and, particularly in the interior, it is tactful to avoid those cafés which obviously belong to the local men. It is not difficult to recognise these *clubs*. The range of drinks in the larger cafés is exactly the same as elsewhere in France. Many of the larger cafés offer a range of elaborate ice-creams with an illustrated menu in full colour.

Shopping

Some people, including many French, still regard Corsica as a remote, uncivilised place. Ajaccio and Bastia are now excellent shopping centres with everything from smart boutiques to large supermarkets. The shops in the smaller towns will provide all your day-to-day needs. If you are staying in one of the remoter resorts there will be basic shopping and excursions to larger towns. There are souvenir shops everywhere and in the larger towns shops specialising in Corsican foods, wines and liqueurs.

Health

It is safe to drink the water everywhere unless specifically advised against it.

The island is covered by an efficient medical and ambulance

service and Ajaccio and Bastia have large hospitals. In case of extreme emergency you would be flown to the mainland.

I noticed excellent chemists' shops everywhere but you would be wise to take the necessary supply of any medicines requiring a doctor's prescription.

Books about Corsica

Please see the 'Select Bibliography' at the end of the book. There are no recent guide-books to Corsica in English but the *Guide Bleu* and the *Michelin Guide* are excellent but they are not written in simple French. You will find a small dictionary useful for them and for other occasions. The Corsicans have their own language, strongly influenced by Italian. Everyone the visitor is likely to meet will speak French though on occasions the strong local accent may make it difficult to understand. However, in the world of tourism, many of the people you will deal with were not born in Corsica.

A Suggested Itinerary Around Corsica

Introduction

The most interesting places in Corsica are scattered all over the island and because of the great complex of mountains that occupy the centre it is not easy to plan an itinerary including all the best places without doubling back on your tracks. The following itinerary avoids that and includes the great majority of places that the average visitor will wish to see.

The itinerary can be adapted to your particular needs, time and tastes. If, for example, you arrive in Corsica at Ajaccio, you start using the itinerary from the 9th day and work forward from there. If you are going to visit Ajaccio, Bastia and Bonifacio, you use those sections and ignore the rest. I have suggested a leisurely 18-day tour of the island. The itinerary could certainly be compressed to 14 days but with less than two weeks you would find you spent most of your time driving to cover the whole of this route. But it is easy to use that part of the itinerary that fits your timetable.

The itinerary is based on the Michelin map of Corsica, Sheet 90, which is essential for touring Corsica. I have divided my notes into three sections. First there is a description of the day's route with basic directions and road numbers which are simple to follow with the Michelin map. I have listed the main attractions and given one star to everything which I think it is worth making an effort to see. Some starred items are more important than others but a graded star-system involves personal taste so I decided to leave the reader to choose his/her own preferences. My own favourites will be obvious from the main text which should be used in conjunction with the itinerary. At all times use this itinerary in conjunction with the full index which will interlock the main text with these brief notes.

Second, I have given a brief note on driving conditions for each section of the route. Most road surfaces in Corsica are satisfactory but some of the white roads on the Michelin map are poor. The main problem is inadequate signposting and on complicated routes the person map-reading must remain alert all the time.

Finally, I have given a brief description of the hotels we stayed at during our tour in the autumn of 1986. The 'star' rating is based on that given in the 1983 *Guide Bleu*. Corsican hotels listed in the *Michelin Rouge* are limited but all places with a Michelin recommendation are underlined in red on the Michelin map. It will be obvious from these notes, and in certain cases from longer comments in the main text, which hotels I would particularly recommend. Although we used only one- and two-star hotels, there are grander hotels in the large towns and resorts. All the hotels I've listed are likely to be open in the spring and autumn.

1ST DAY: BASTIA
(pp. 19–33)

TERRA-VECCHIA: Place St-Nicholas: Place de l'Hôtel de Ville: St-Jean-Baptiste: Chapelle de l'Immaculée Conception*: Chapelle St-Roch: Vieux-Port*: Jardin Romieu.

TERRA-NOVA: La Citadelle: Musée d'Ethnographie corse: Ste-Marie: Chapelle Ste-Croix*.

Driving: Traffic is heavy and parking difficult. The old town is best seen on foot.

Hotel: *Coin de la Corniche** (restaurant). San-Martino-di-Lota. T.95.31.40.98. There are several hotels in Bastia but we preferred this simple hotel in a magnificent position in the mountains north of the town. It is 13 km from Bastia and about a 25-min drive. Drive either north along the coast road D 80 and turn left up the D 31 at Miomo or take the D 231 from the centre of Bastia and pick up the other end of the D 31 over the mountains. It is likely to be heavily booked in summer. The food was adequate but not exciting.

2ND DAY: BASTIA TO CENTURI-PORT (60 KM)
(pp. 34–44)

Bastia to San-Martino-di-Lota* (view) by D 31 and down to main coast road D 80: Erbalunga* (port, Genoese tower):

174 A Suggested Itinerary Around Corsica

Marine de Sisco (Eglise de Ste-Catherine): Rogliano (view, fortified villages): Ersa (circuit by D 253 and D 153 to N promontory): Barcaggio (view, Island of la Giraglia, Genoese tower): return to Ersa on D 153: continue along D 80 to Col de Serra* (view, Moulin Mattei): Centuri-Port* (fishing port) down from D 80 by D 35.

Driving: Easy, winding coast road with steep tracks at northern tip of Cap Corse.

Hotel: *Vieux Moulin** (restaurant). Centuri-Port. T. 95.35.60.15. Attractive position with a garden overlooking the port. Some rooms in an annexe at end of garden. The restaurant is popular so book a table for dinner on arrival. Good food and erratic service.

3RD DAY: CENTURI-PORT TO SAN PELLEGRINO (114 KM)
(pp. 45–47 and 52–57)

Follow D 80 south to Pino (port, Franciscan friary): excursion inland here on D 180 to Col de Ste-Lucie* and Tour de Sénèque (view): return to D 80 and south through Marinca (old asbestos plant): Nonza* (rock, Genoese tower, Ste-Julie): take D 81 to Patrimonio* (view of town and St-Nicolas, famous wine area): Col de Teghime* (view): Bastia, where take N 193 going south with view of Etang de Biguglia to the left: take D 507 signposted to Bastia airport and follow the road around the southern end of the airport to Mariana (Roman ruins): La Canonica* (Pisan church): 300 m SW San Parteo (Pisan church): return to N 193, then continue south along N 198: after 1 km turn left at Folelli onto D 506 to San Pellegrino.

Driving: Good but slowish roads to Bastia. Fast road from Bastia to San Pellegrino with adequate minor roads. Watch carefully for the airport turning.

Hotel: *San Pellegrino*** (restaurant). San Pellegrino. T. 95.36.90.61. This is a pleasant, modern resort hotel by the sea with rooms in separate cabins. It is convenient for sightseeing in this area out of season but is likely to be fully booked during the summer. Pleasant dining room with good food and pleasant service.

A Suggested Itinerary Around Corsica 175

4TH DAY: SAN PELLEGRINO TO CORTE (175 KM)
(pp. 48–52 and 57–62)

From San Pellegrino, return to N 198, drive N: at Casamozza turn left onto N 193: at Ponte Leccia take D 71 to Morosaglia* (Paoli birthplace museum, beginning of chestnut forests, the Castagniccia area): Orezza friary* (ruins): on the left the turning to Orezza mineral spring: the beautiful D 71 carries on to Cervione and reaches the coast at Prunete where you turn south on N 198 to Aleria* (Greek and Roman museum, Genoese fort, the site of Roman Aleria): return to N 198, turn left and at first major crossroads turn left on N 200 to Corte, an attractive road following the Tavignano river.

Driving: The main roads are excellent. The roads through the Castagniccia are narrow and slow with the hazard of pigs and cows in the road. The views all the way are beautiful.

Hotel: *Hôtel de la Paix*** (restaurant). Place du Duc de Padoue, Corte. T. 95.46.06.72. A gloomy but comfortable hotel in the middle of the modern town where we had an excellent dinner. We chose this hotel since we arrived too late in Corte to start looking around and our guide-book recommended it as the best central hotel. The next day we found a pleasanter hotel outside Corte which made a perfect base for our stay:

*Auberg de la Restonica** (restaurant). Corte. T. 95.46.09.58. The hotel is about 3 km along the D 623, on the left at the mouth of the Gorges de la Restonica. Quiet, with pleasant rooms and a large garden, the food was excellent. It is advisable to telephone in advance.

5TH DAY: CORTE AND THE GORGES DE LA RESTONICA (30 KM)
(pp. 104–123)

LA VILLE HAUTE*: Place Paoli: Place Gaffori (maison de Gaffori): Eglise de l'Annonciation: Place Poilu (Bonaparte house, Palais National): La Citadelle*: Belvédère* (view). Good view of the citadel from below by the Pont Tavignano. There is nothing of interest in the modern town.

Gorges de la Restonica*, leave Corte by the D 623 south and drive though the gorges as far as Bergeries de Grotelle* (view). From here there are footpaths to the neighbouring lakes and mountains.

Driving: The Ville Haute of Corte must be seen on foot. The road through the Gorges de la Restonica is slow with a poor surface.

Hotel: *Auberge de la Restonica*, 2nd night.

6TH DAY: CORTE, EXCURSIONS TO HAUT-ASCO AND CANTON OF SERMANO (152 KM)
(*pp. 121–122 and 149*)

Drive north along N 193 to Ponte Leccia and fork left onto N 197. After 2 km turn left onto D 47 which becomes the D 147 at the beginning of the Gorges de l'Asco* (view): Asco: Pont génois: Forêt de Carrozzica*: Haut-Asco* (view of Mt Cinto, winter sports centre). Turn back to Ponte Leccia.

The drive through the Canton of Sermano is a most attractive alternative route back to Corte. 5 km south of Ponte Leccia along the N 193 turn left onto the D 39 to San Lorenzo: then by the D 15 to Cambia, Carticasi and Bustanico: D 441 to Sermano: take the D 41 south-westward, turn right at Féo onto the D 14 and you will meet the N 200 which brings you back to Corte.

Driving: The D 147 through the gorges and to Haut-Asco is narrow, winding and often steep but a reasonable surface. The route through the canton of Sermano is all on winding minor roads where it is easy to miss your turnings unless you keep your eye on your map. The roads are better than the signposting.

Hotel: *Auberge de la Restonica*, 3rd night.

7TH DAY: CORTE TO PORTO (97 KM)
(*pp. 124–135*)

From the north of Corte take the D 18 and you meet the D 84, turn left. This road narrows into the Scala di Santa Regina* (view): Calacuccia* (view across lake): Forêt de Valdo-Niello*: Col de Vergio* (view): Forêt d'Aitone*: Evisa: Gorges de Spelunca* (extraordinary rock formations): Porto: Marine de Porto (position and views).

Driving: Care must be taken all through the narrow, winding mountain route where there seemed to be more traffic coming around the blind corners from the opposite direction.

Hotel: *Soleil Couchant** (restaurant). Marine de Porto. T. 95.26.10.12. A small, simple hotel on the edge of the south of the port. It has a terrace restaurant and the food is simple but excellent but one is free to eat in all the other restaurants of the port.

8TH DAY: PORTO TO AJACCIO (84 KM)
(pp. 128–134)

In the morning I recommend the boat excursion out through the Golfe de Porto* (view of pink granite cliffs): on to the nature reserve of La Scandola* (view, birdlife, sea grottoes and rock formations): lunch at Girolata, small port with Genoese tower only accessible by sea: return to Porto.

Afternoon drive to Ajaccio. Take D 81 south along the coast from Porto. This road goes through les Calanches* (dramatic pink rock cliff formations): to Piana* (view): continue down D 81 with a fine view of the Golfe de Sagone to the right: you meet the N 194 which soon brings you to the N 193 on the outskirts of Ajaccio. Follow signposts to the centre of the town.

Driving: The first part of the road through les Calanches needs care but there are places at the best viewpoints for parking. Later the road is easy and reasonably fast.

Hotel: *Spunta di Mare*** (restaurant). Ajaccio. T. 95.22.41.42. Again, we looked for a hotel out of the noisy centre of the town. This hotel is on the southern outskirts. Drive east from town centre following the signposts to the airport on N 193 and about 1 km from the junction with N 194, turn sharp-left up a steep road and the hotel is on the right. Pleasant rooms and excellent, simple food. The restaurant is closed on Sundays but there are good restaurants nearby. Even in mid-October the hotel was full. Book in advance by telephone.

9TH DAY: AJACCIO
(pp. 92–103)

Jetée de la Citadelle* (view of port and golfe d'Ajaccio): Citadelle (outside only): Église St-Érasme: Musée du Capitellu: Cathédrale (font where Napoleon baptised): Maison Bonaparte* (Napoleon's birthplace): Place Maréchal-Foch: Musée Napoléonien: Chapelle impériale: Musée Fesch* (part of the collection of Cardinal Fesch; important Italian paintings. The museum was closed for renovation in 1986 and may remain closed for two more years.): Iles Sanguinaires can be seen either by a boat excursion from the port, or by driving westwards to the end of the D 111 to the Pointe de la Parata* (fine view at sunset).

Seeing Ajaccio is best divided between the 9th day and the morning of the 10th day.

Driving: Parking is difficult in the old town and it is easier to walk around this area.

Hotel: *Spunta di Mare*, 2nd night.

10TH DAY: AJACCIO TO PORTO-POLLO (90 KM)
(pp. 79–83)

Take N 196 eastwards to Cauro where the road turns south to the northern side of the Golfe de Valinco. Turn right onto the D 157 and after 9 km follow signposts along minor road D 57 to Station Préhistorique de Filitosa* (menhirs, main settlement, museum): return on same road for 4 km and turn right on D 157. After 1 km turn left onto D 757 and follow through to Porto-Pollo (view).

Driving: Mainly good roads but a little rough around Filitosa.

Hotel: *Le Golfe** (restaurant 100 m away). Porto-Pollo. T. 95.74.01.66. An extremely simple but clean and comfortable hotel in a quiet position. When we arrived in mid-October it was the only hotel in the area still open. The restaurant was excellent; breakfast on a terrace overlooking the gulf. An ideal base for Filitosa which is only twenty-five minutes' drive away.

11TH DAY: PORTO-POLLO TO SARTÈNE (47 KM)
(pp. 83–86)

Return via the D 757 and the D 157 to the main road, the N 196, where you turn right. After 5 km you can turn to visit the port and seaside resort of Propriano: the D 557 to the left leads in 3 km to the thermal baths of the Bains de Baracci: continuing south on N 196, in about 7 km turn left onto the D 268 and in just over 4 km on your left, crossing the Rizzanèse river is the old Genoese stone bridge, Spin' A Cavallu* (the best in Corsica): turn back along the D 268 and after 3.5 km turn left onto the D 69 and climb 6 km to Sartène.

VIEILLE VILLE: Place de la Libération* (view): Eglise Ste-Marie* (cross and chains of the *Catenacciu*): Hôtel de Ville: Quartier de Santa Anna* (intriguing old quarter).

Musée de Préhistoire corse* (housed in the old prison): 5 km east of the town on the D 65 the Belvédère de Foce* (view).

Driving: An easy drive. In Sartène sightseeing must be done on foot.

Hotel: *Les Roches*** (restaurant). Sartène. T. 95.77.07.61.

Excellent hotel on the north-eastern edge of town looking over the deep valley and well placed for sightseeing. The rooms are adequate, the service and the food excellent. It is popular with groups, even in late October, so it would be wise to telephone in advance. You will probably need two nights in Sartène.

12TH DAY: SURROUNDINGS OF SARTÈNE (90 KM)
(pp 87–91)

I would recommend a morning excursion to the 'vendetta country' to the north-east of Sartène, returning to the town for lunch and in the afternoon making an excursion to the megalithic sites to the south-west.

The north-east excursion: Take the D 69 back to the D 268 and turn right. In 4.5 km turn left onto the D 69 but immediately after crossing the river Rizzanèse, turn left onto a minor road, the D 119 and afterwards the D 19, which will bring you to Santa Maria Figaniella* (Pisan church): return along same road, D 19, to the village of Fozzano* (scene of the famous vendetta which inspired Mérimée's *Colomba*): return by same route to Sartène.

For the southern excursion to two megalithic sites, leave Sartène on the N 196 and after 2.5 km turn right onto the minor road D 48. In 9 km turn left onto a track-road D 48A following signs to Cauria. Drive as far as you are allowed, then leave car and walk about 1 km to the megalithic site* (finest dolmen in Corsica, menhirs). Drive back to D 48, turn left and drive for 2 km where to the right is a rough track signposted to Alignement de Palaggiu* (menhirs): return to D 48 and turning right the road will bring you to the sea and the small port of Tizzano (view): direct return drive to Sartène takes only 35 minutes.

Driving: Slow, winding roads all the way with rough tracks leading to the megalithic sites.

Hotel: *Les Roches*, 2nd night.

13TH DAY: SARTÈNE TO BONIFACIO (55 KM)
(*pp. 67–78*)

Drive south on the N 196: in 23 km the pass of Roccapina* (view, lion-rock, Genoese tower): Bonifacio* which is divided into three parts, the port, the old town, the citadel.

THE OLD PORT* (view, boat excursions* from the quay: aquarium): steps leading to Col St-Roch (view) and through the Portes de Gênes into the VIEILLE VILLE*: Place d'Armes: Rue des Deux Empereurs: Eglise Ste-Marie Majeure: Escalier du Roi d'Aragon: beyond the old town the CITADEL: Foreign Legion monument: main barracks (closed to the public): to the left of the barracks St-Dominique*: beyond the barracks ruined mills and towers, the remains of the friary of St-Francis and a large cemetery: good views of the harbour all along the ramparts.

Excursions near Bonifacio: leave town by the D 58 and take first turning right, in 5 km Phare de Pertusato* (view): take main road N 198 north and N 196 westward, then first left to Ermitage de la Trinité* (view). The boat excursion from the port for the sea view of the town and the visit to grottoes is worthwhile.

Driving: Main roads reasonable. Local roads poor.

Hotel: *Étrangers** (no restaurant out of summer season). Bonifacio. T. 95.73.01.09. About 1 km north of the town on the left of the N 198. Adequate rooms and good breakfast. Suggest you avoid the small restaurant slightly up the road on the right. There are several restaurants along the quay of the old port.

14TH DAY: BONIFACIO TO COL DE BAVELLA TO PORTO-VECCHIO (185 KM)
(pp 88–89)

Leave Bonifacio by N 198 and turn left onto N 196 and in 13 km turn right onto D 859 signposted to airport. After 11 km turn left onto D 59 and drive north to Carbini* (Pisan church, birthplace of the Giovannali heresy): drive to Levie and take D 268 west to Ste-Lucie-de-Tallano* (view, church): return to Levie and follow D 268 north through Zonza to the Col de Bavella* (view, fine 80-min walk around the col with superb views): drive on through pine forêt de Bavella: Col de Larone* (view): the D 268 brings you out on the east coast at Solenzara where you turn south onto the N 198. You can either drive straight through this main road to Porto-Vecchio or go by way of the following attractive diversion. Drive down N 198 for 25.5 km, pass village of Pirelli and imediately after crossing the small Cavo river at Ste-Lucie-de-Porto-Vecchio turn left down D 168A until you come to Pinarello facing a gulf. Take the D 468 south following along the northern coast of the Golfe de Porto-Vecchio until you meet the N 198 again and turn left when you reach Porto-Vecchio* (port, old fortifications).

Driving: The mountain roads are slow and in places poorly surfaced.

Hotel: *San Giovanni*** (no restaurant out of season) near Porto-Vecchio. T. 95.70.22.25. To the south-west of Porto-Vecchio, leaving on the N 198 and shortly turning right onto the D 659 to Arca; the hotel entrance is about 3 km on the left. A quiet, charming hotel built in a cork forest with attractive garden and comfortable rooms. Their restaurant had closed for the winter but the owner recommended an excellent restaurant 3 km away. Excellent breakfast in the hotel. It would be wise to telephone in advance; in season the hotel must be popular and out of season I felt they might suddenly decide to close the hotel. I thought the hotel preferable to the noisy, rather claustrophobic atmosphere of the town.

15TH DAY: PORTO-VECCHIO THROUGH CENTRAL MOUNTAINS TO BASTELICA (194 KM)
(pp. 149–153)

Take the D 368 westwards to climb through the Forêt de l'Ospédale* (view back to coast): pass a large lake and continue to Zonza with mountain views all the way: crossing the D 268, take the D 420 through the villages of Quenza, Serra-di-Scopamène to Aullène: drive north on D 69 over Col de la Vaccia* (view) and on to Zicavo, through the Forêt de S Pietro di Verde, over the Col de Verde and down into the valley to Ghisoni* (view of famous rocks): leave Ghisoni still on D 69 and in 20 km over the Col de Sorba you reach the main N 193 where you turn left towards Ajaccio, just south of Vivario. Drive southwards through Vizzavona, over the Col de Vizzavona* (view) and through the village of Bocognano. About 7 km after the village turn left onto D 127 and D 27, a *difficult* minor road, through Tavera to Bastelica* (birthplace of Sampiero Corso).

Driving: A long, tiring but most rewarding drive all the way although you may have rain and low cloud in the mountains in October. Road surfaces are reasonable all the way until the last section on the D 27 after the D 127 to Bastelica where the surface deteriorates into a pot-holed, rutted ruin but was passable with care. Do not try to go to Bastelica on the D 27 immediately south of Bocognano on the N 193. Although it is signposted to Bastelica it disappears into an old landslide after about 3 km. Unless you look with extreme care at the Michelin map you will not see that this dead end is faithfully recorded.

Hotel: *U Castagnetu*** (restaurant). Bastelica. T. 95.28.70.71. Situated above the village in a peaceful position with views across the valley. A comfortable hotel (closed November) with exceptionally good restaurant and breakfast on the terrace. This hotel is popular with local people and it would be wise to telephone and make a booking.

16TH DAY: BASTELICA TO CALVI (194 KM)
(*pp. 133–134*)

Leave Bastelica southwards on the D 27 and after about 4 km turn right onto the narrow D 3 which runs along the north side of the dam and through the Gorges du Prunelli* (view): the D 3 eventually meets the N 196 where you turn right and join the N 193. After 3.5 km turn left onto the N 194 and after 3 km turn right onto the D 81 going northwards towards Cargèse* (Greek Orthodox church and community). Continue along the D 81 through Piana* (view of les Calanche) and through Porto. The D 81 climbs up to the Col de Croix and afterwards to the Col de Palmarella* (view): follow the D 81 until it meets the D 351, turn left and in 2 km turn right, cross the Fango river and take the D 51. You will meet the D 251 where you turn left until you reach the N 197 which will bring you into the port of Calvi.

Driving: A slow road most of the way but beautiful and varied scenery.

Hotel: *Méditerranée*** (restaurant). Calvi. T. 95.65.08.58. On the north-west edge of the town, convenient for the port and the citadel, a comfortable, package tour hotel. The restaurant looked characterless but there are several good restaurants nearby and several other hotels in Calvi and out along the beach.

17TH DAY: CALVI TO L'ILE-ROUSSE TO ST-FLORENT (70 KM)
(pp. 136–144)

CALVI, LA CITADELLE*: Genoese citadel and old town: the fortifications (best view from port): entrance to citadel across Place Christophe-Colomb: Governor's Palace: St-Jean-Baptiste: Oratoire de la confrérie St-Antoine: Maison Pacciola: Palais Giubega.

LA MARINE*: The old port, like the citadel, is a model of sensible conservation and planning to cope with the tourist invasion. The port (view to citadel): Tour du Sel: Ste-Marie-Majeure.

Leave Calvi by the N 197 through Lumio (view of gulf): in 24 km you reach l'Ile-Rousse, the town founded by Pasquale Paoli in the eighteenth century: Place Paoli: Vieille Ville to north: Ile de la Pietra and port* (view).

Follow the N 197 and the D 81 to St-Florent: Vieille Ville* (Genoese citadel): port: Sta-Maria Assunta* (Pisan church 1 km east of town).

Driving: A tortuous road but interesting scenery.

Hotel: *Hotel Santa Maria*** (no restaurant). St-Florent. T. 95.37.04.44. Situated at the north-east entrance to the town on the D 81. A modern, comfortable hotel and convenient for sightseeing. Good breakfast. There are several good restaurants in the town. The hotel recommends *La Marinuccia* which was excellent and reasonable.

18TH DAY: ST-FLORENT TO BASTIA (23 KM)

Follow D 81 through Patrimonio and over the Col de Teghime to Bastia. If you wish to take a ferry from Ajaccio, the drive from Bastia takes 4 hours on the N 193.

Select Bibliography

There are not a large number of books in English about Corsica and the earlier books of the eighteenth and nineteenth centuries will normally be found only in a good library. I hope the general reader will find this short list useful. I have added brief notes where I think books will be of particular interest.

FOR THE TRAVELLER

Guide Bleu, *Corse*, Hachette, 1983.
Michelin, *Carte de Corse*, Sheet 90, Michelin, 1986.
Michelin, Guide de Tourisme, *Corse*, Michelin, 1985.
Michelin, *Guides rouges hôteliers – France*, Michelin, 1986.
Collomb, R., *Corsica Mountains*, West Col, 1982. (Essential for mountaineers, climbers and walkers.)
Wager, G., *Your Guide to Corsica*, Alvin Redman, 1965.

INTERPRETATION

Carrington, D., *Granite Island: A Portrait of Corsica*, Longman, 1971; Penguin, 1984.
(This is a brilliant interpretation of Corsican history, life, traditional culture. It is not a guide-book but wherever you go in the island the book will increase your understanding.)

FURTHER READING

Benson, R., *Sketches of Corsica*, London, 1825.
Boswell, J., *An Account of Corsica, the Journal of a Tour to that Island and Memoirs of Pascal Paoli*, London, 1768.
Boswell, J. (ed. M. Bishop), *The Journal of a Tour to Corsica and Memoirs of Pascal Paoli*, Williams & Norgate, 1951.
Campbell, T., *Southward Ho!*, London, 1868.
Elliot, E., *Life and Letters of Sir Gilbert Elliot*, 3 vols (vol 2 Corsica), London, 1874.
Elwell, C., *Corsican Excursion*, The Bodley Head, 1954.
Gregorvious, F., *Corsica in its Picturesque, Social and Historical Aspects . . .* , London, 1855.
Lear, E., *Journal of a Landscape Painter in Corsica*, London, 1870.
McLaren, M., *Corsican Boswell*, Secker & Warburg, 1966.
Merriman, H., *The Isle of Unrest*, London, 1899.
Pirie, V., *His Majesty of Corsica*, William Collins, 1939.
Renwick, G. *Romantic Corsica*, Fisher Unwin, 1909.
Thrasler, P., *Pasquale Paoli*, Constable, 1970.

NOVELS ABOUT CORSICA

Daudet, A., sketches and stories in *Lettres de Mon Moulin*, Paris, 1869, and *Etudes et Paysages*, Paris, 1874.
Dumas, A., *Les Frères Corses*, Paris, 1845.
Mérimée, P., *Colomba*, Paris, 1845. (Published in Penguin Classics but now out of print.)

Index

Aboukir, battle of, 29
Abro, 174
Agriates, Désert des, 141
Aitone, Forêt d', 126, 148, 177
Ajaccio, 22, 23, 30, 33, 46, 50, 63,
    92–103, 107, 134, 151, 157, 177–8
  cathedral, 100–1
  Chapelle impériale, 97, 178
  citadel, 99, 178
  cours Napoléon, 93
  Fesch museum, 96–7, 178
  fountain of Four Lions, 98
  Gulf of Ajaccio, 101–3, 178
  Hôtel de Ville, 98–9
  Iles Sanguinaires, 93, 102–3, 178
  Jetée de la Citadelle, 101, 178
  musée du Capitellu, 100, 178
  musée Napoléonien, 98–9
  Napoleon's birthplace, 94–5, 99, 178
  old port, 101
  Place Maréchal-Foch, 98, 99
  Punta Guardiola, 93
  Pointe de la Parata, 103, 178
  ruê Cardinal Fesch, 97
  St-Érasme, 100, 178
  St-Roch, 97
  Ste-Croix, 100
  statue of Napoleon, 98
  tourist office, 99
Alalia, 49
Aléria, 46, 49–53, 109
Alfonso V, king of Aragon, 71–3, 105, 137
Algajola, 22, 108, 140
Algeria (*see* North Africa)
Alice in Wonderland, 128

America, 48, 112, 116
amianthus, 46
Annapurna, 164
aperitifs, Corsican, 168
Arabs, 11, 63, 64, 98
Arles, 20
asbestos, 46
Asco, Gorges de l', 121, 149, 176
Asuka, Japan, 91
Athos, Mount, 134
Auchinleck, Lord (Boswell's father), 110
Aullène, 182
Australia, 131

Bacciochi, Elisa, 100
Bach, Pierre, 37
Bali, island of, 14
Baltimore, 153
Baracci, Bains de, 179
Barbary pirates, 10, 53, 84
Barcaggio, 41
Bardon, Marc, 37
Bartoli, Colomba, 87–8
Bastelica, 106, 151–3, 183
Bastia, 19–33, 36, 43, 46, 47, 48, 53,
    63, 99, 109, 113, 114, 136, 153,
    157, 173, 184
  bandstand, 22
  Boulevard Paoli, 32
  Chapelle Ste-Croix, 31
  Chapelle de l'Immaculée Conception, 28
  Chapelle St-Roche, 28
  Ethnographical museum, 29
  Genose citadel, 21, 22, 27, 28–30
  history, 22–3

Bastia (*contd*)
  Jardin Romieu, 27
  Jetée du Dragon, 27
  modern development, 23
  name, origin of, 23
  new port, 21
  old port, 21, 27–8
  Place de la Hôtel-de-Ville, 26
  Place Guasco, 31
  Place St-Nicholas, 21, 23
  Rue des Terrasses, 28
  Rue Napoléon, 28
  Ste-Marie, 28, 30–1
  St-Jean-Baptiste, 26–7
  statue of Napoleon, 22
  Terra-Nova, 28, 30–2
  Terra-Vecchia, 26
Bavella, Col de, 181
beach holidays, 157–8
Beau Geste, 76
Benedictines, 45
Birmingham, 153
Bizet, 22
Bocognano, 151, 182–3
Bonaparte, Carlo, 93–5, 97, 112, 118
Bonaparte, Joseph, 96, 118
Bonaparte, Letizia, 93–5, 97
Bonaparte, Napoleon, 23, 35, 64, 68, 74, 92–7, 101, 106, 112
  baptism, 100
  birth, 92
  birthplace, 94–5
  Brienne, 95
  Cardinal Fesch (step-uncle), 95–6
  Comte de Marbeuf, 94
  Ecole Militaire, 95
  Egypt, 93
  Florentine ancestors, 94
  Italian campaign, 94
  Les Invalides, 95
  Musée Napoléonien, 98–9
  nickname, 94
  Paris, 95
  St Helena, 95, 101
Bonifacio, 12, 22, 48, 67–78, 99, 105, 136–7, 180–1
  barracks, 75
  Cavallo island, 77
  cemetery, 76–7
  Charles V, 68, 74
  citadel, 67, 68, 70, 71–7
  Count Bonifacio, 70
  Escalier du roi d'Aragon, 75
  French siege, 73
  French Foreign Legion, 75–6
  Genoese, 70
  Giola, 70
  Grotte de St-Antoine, 77
  Grotte du Sdragonata, 77
  Gulf of Sta Manza, 77
  history, 70–4
  Napoleon, 68
  old port, 68–9, 74
  old town, 74–5
  Pertusato lighthouse, 77
  Porte de Gênes, 74
  relic of the True Cross, 67–8
  St-Dominique, 76
  Ste-Marie-Majeure, 74–5
  St-Julian, 68, 76
  Sardinia car-ferry, 69, 74
  sea excursions, 69, 77
  sieges, 71–4
  Spanish siege, 71–3
Boswell, James, 34, 42–3, 44, 59, 60
  Berlin, 42
  Harwich, 42
  Johnson, Samuel, 42, 110–111
  Journal of a Tour to Corsica, 110
  Leghorn, 43
  meeting with Paoli, 110–12
  Rome, 43
  Sienna, 43,
  Turin, 43
  Utrecht, 42
  Voltaire, 42
  Wilkes, 43
Botticelli, 96
boule, game of, 143–4
Brando, 38
Britain, 16, 92, 93, 95, 109, 111, 114, 116, 137
  Anglo-Corsican Viceroyalty, 114–16
Buddha, 86
Burney, Fanny, 111

bus excursions, 155, 157
Bustanico, 122, 176
Byron, Lord, 138
Byzantine empire, 53

cafés, 170
Calacuccia, 177
Calanche, les, 125, 133, 134, 154, 183
Calatrava, Knights of, 138
Calvi, 12, 22, 70, 71, 99, 136–40, 153, 157, 183–4
   Christopher Columbus, 138
   citadel, 136, 139
   Don Juan, 138
   history, 137
   Lord Nelson, 137
   motto and arms, 137, 139
   old port, 136, 140
   Palais des Gouverneurs, 139
   Place Christophe-Colomb, 137–8
   Rue Clemenceau, 140
   Ste-Marie, 140
   St-Jean-Baptiste, 139
Campbell, Miss Thomasina, 92
Cambia, 176
Canari, 46
Canonica, La (Sta-Maria-Assunta), 54–7, 142–3
Cap Corse, 20–1, 34–47
Capitello, lake, 123
car and passenger ferries, 19, 156, 159–60
Carabelli family, 87–8
Carbini, 88–9, 181
Carcopino, Jérôme, 52
   museum (Aleria), 52
Cardo, 23
Cargèse, 133–4, 183
   Argentinian nettle-trees, 134
   Golfe de Sagone, 133
   Greek colony, 133–4
   Greek Orthodox church, 133–4
   Marbeuf, 134
Carrington, Dorothy, 18, 114, 138
Caro river, 181
Carrozzica, Forét de, 176
Carthaginians, 49
Carticasi, 176

Casamozza, 175
Casabianca, 29, 30
Castagniccia, 57–62, 122
Cateau-Cambrésis, treaty of, 107
Cattaciolo, Dominique, 73
Cauria, Mégalithes de, 89–90, 180
Cauro, 178
Ceccaldi, Andrea, 108
Centuri, 42–4, 157
Cervione, 175
Charlemagne, 53
Charles V, Emperor, 68, 74, 106
Charles VI, Emperor, 108
Chemins de Fer Corse, 141, 153, 164, 4
Chiostro, Capo au, 122
Christe Eleison rock, 150
Cinarchesi families, 105–6
Cinto, Monte, 126, 148, 149, 176
Claudius, Emperor, 45
climbing, 164
Collomb, Robert, 164
Colomba, 87–8, 180
Colombus, Christopher, 137–8
Conrad, Joseph, 80
Corse de Sud, 23
Corsica
   agriculture, 12, 48, 49, 50, 58
   food and cooking, 58, 62, 153
   history, 11–12, 48–53, 60–1, 62–6
   landscape, 16, ch. 10
   language, 66
   modern politics, 62–6
   people, 16, 19–20, 49, 53
   traditional life, 17, 29, 58–9, 83, 87–8, 105
   vendetta, 87–8
Corso, Sampiero, 11, 73, 106, 108, 182
   birth, 106, 151
   life, 106–7
   statue, 152
Corte, 13, 16, 43, 60, 61, 93, 104–19, 122, 175
   Belvédère, 119, 175
   Blaire du Signori (St-Theophil), 117–8
   citadel, 104, 105, 118, 175
   Corsican capital, 104

Corte (contd)
  Cours Paoli, 117
  Église de l'Annonciation, 117, 175
  history, 104–16
  old town, 104
  Palais National, 118
  Place du Duc de Padoue, 175
  Place du Poilu (Bonaparte's home), 118, 175
  Place Gaffori, 117, 175
  Place Paoli, 117, 175
  Pont Tavignano, 104, 119, 175
  Restonica river, 119, 123
  St-Jean, 104
  statue of Gaffori, 117, 119
  statue of Paoli, 117
  Tavignano river, 119
  university, 45, 66, 117, 118
Cosimo Tura, 96
Country Life, 148
Croix, Col de, 183
Cursay, Marquis de, 110

Daibertus, Archbishop of Pisa, 54
Delacroix, Eugène, 100
Dien Bien Phu, 62
Dila dai Monti, 58, 105
Diqua dai Monti, 58, 105
distances in Corsica, 162
dolmens, 81, 90, 91
Dominicans, 45, 76
Dragut (Turkish pirate), 73, 106
Durazzo family, 87–8

Egypt, 93
Elliot, Lady, 114
Elliot, Sir Gilbert (later Baron Minto), 114–16
Erbalunga, 34, 37–8,
  La Cerca procession, 38
  La Granitola procession, 38
Ersa, 41, 42
Etang de Biguglia, 174
Etang de Diane, 49
Etruscans, 49, 137
Evisa, 126, 148, 177

Fango river, 183

Féo, 176
ferry routes, 159–60
Fesch, Cardinal Joseph, 95–7, 100
  Ajaccio Academy, 96
  Archbishop of Lyons, 96
  Chapelle impériale, 95, 97
  Fesch museum, 96–7
  Italian primitives, 96
  Joseph Bonaparte, 96
  Napoleon's step-uncle, 95
  painting collection, 95, 96
  will, 96, 97
Filitosa, 80–3, 91, 178–9
  site museum, 83
fishing, 145–7
Flaubert, Gustave, 107
FLNC (see *Front de libération nationale de la Corse*)
fly/drive, 160
Folelli, 174
Fontanaccia, Dolmen of, 90, 91
food, 164–6
Fourth Crusade, 76
Fozzano, 87–8, 180
France, 16, 24, 43, 60, 64, 93, 95, 106, 107, 109, 110, 112, 113, 114, 116, 137
Francis of Assisi, Saint, 68, 77
Franciscans, 43, 45, 61, 68, 89, 112, 117–8
French Foreign Legion, 75–6, 77
French Indo-China, 62–3
French Revolution, 61, 95, 100, 113, 116
French Tourist Authority, 17, 97, 99, 155, 164
  London address, 155
Front de libération nationale de la Corse (FLNC) 11–12, 16–17, 44, 64–6, 102
Fuji, Mount, 141

Gaffori, General Gian' Pietro, 109, 110
  house, 117
  statue, 117, 119
  wife's courage, 117
garages, 163

Genoa
  Ajaccio, 99
  agricultural policy, 58–9
  Bonifacio, 67–8, 70
  bridges, 86, 146, 148
  Calvi, 137, 139
  citadels, 24–5
  Corte, 105, 106, 117
  Greek immigrants, 133
  history, 22–3
  l'Ile-Rousse, 140
  Independence movement, 60–1, 108, 113, 118
  Miguel Manara, 138
  Pisa loses to Genoa, 54
  Rule of Corsica, 11, 16
  Sampiero Corso, 107
  Sartène, 84
  treaty with France, 43, 93, 109–10
Genoese towers and forts
  Aleria, 52
  Erbalunga, 38
  Girolta, 131
  Nonza, 46
  Porto, 127
Gérard (painter), 98, 99
Ghisoni, 150–1, 182
Giafferi, Luigi, 108
Gilbert & Sullivan, 114
Giola, 70
Giovannali heretics, 89
Giraglia island, 41
Girolta, 130–1, 177
Golo river, 52–3
Gounod, 22
Greeks, 11, 48–52, 62, 137
  Alalia, 49–50
  ceramics, 50, 52
Gregory the Great, Pope, 53
Gregory VII, Pope, 54
Gregory XII, Pope, 100
Grosjean, Roger, 80, 82
Grottelle, Bergeries de, 122, 176
Guardiola, Punta, 93
Guide Bleu, 14, 15, 17, 38, 119, 139, 168, 169, 171, 173

Halfpenny, William, 77

Haute Corse, 25
health, 170–1
Henry II of France, 73, 106
Homer, 67
Horsham slab, 37
hotels, 157–8, 168–9
  Ajaccio, *Spunta di Mare***, 101–2, 177
  Bastelica, *U Castagnetu***, 152, 183
  Bastia (San-Martino-di-Lota), *Coin de la Corniche**, 36, 173
  Bonifacio, *Étrangers***, 77–8, 181
  Calvi, *Mediterranée***, 183
  Centuri-Port, *Vieux-Moulin**, 44, 174
  Corte, *Hôtel de la Paix*** and *Auberge de la Restonica**, 119–21, 175
  Porto, *Soleil Couchant**, 124, 177
  Porto-Pollo, *Le Golfe**, 79–80, 178
  Porto-Vecchio, *San Giovanni***, 182
  St-Florent, *Santa-Maria***, 141–2, 184
  Sartène, *Les Roches***, 86, 179
  San Pellegrino, *San Pellegrino***, 174
Hugo, Victor, 74

l'Ile-Rousse, 114, 137, 140–1, 153, 184
  Place Paoli, 140
  railway station, 141
immigration, 40, 64
Il Trovatore, 152
individual travel, 158–71
insurance, 160
Ishibutai tomb, Japan, 91
Istria, Vincentello d', 105–6
Italian Girl in Algiers, 30
Italy, 12, 42, 50, 138

Japan, 13, 91, 141
Jesuits, 100
Johnson, Dr Samuel, 42, 110–11
Jones, Tom, 102
Journal of a Landscape Painter in Corsica, 13–14

Kyrie Eleison rock, 150

Laestrygonians, 67
Landolphe, Bishop of Pisa, 54
Larone, Col de, 181
Lear, Edward, 13–14, 48, 71, 92–3
Levie, 181
Lille, 20
liqueurs, Corsican, 168
Lombards, 52
Lomellini, Leonello, 23
'Lost Eldorado', 63
Lumio, 184

Macinaggio, 41
Madagascar, 42
Maglioli, Jérôme, 97
malaria, 48, 53
Manara, Miguel (Don Juan), 138
maps and map reading, 161
maquis, 35, 41–2, 158
Marbeuf, Comte de, 94–5
Mariana, 46, 50, 52–3, 57, 142
Marius, 52
Marmano, Forêt de, 150
Marseilles, 19, 44
    Phocaean colony, 50
Medicis, 106
Menton, 44
Mérimée, Prosper, 49, 80, 87, 180
megalithic civilisation
    Brodgar, Orkney, 81
    Carnac, 91
    Japan, 90–1
    Palestine, 81
    Scandinavia, 81
    Spain, 82
    Stonehenge, 81, 83
megalithic culture in Corsica, 80–3, 89–91
megalithic people, 11
Melo, lake, 123
Meloria, battle of, 22
menhirs, 80, 83, 90
Michelin publications
    map of Corsica, Sheet 90, 16, 151, 161–2, 168, 172

    Corse ('green guide') 18, 171
    Guide Rouge, 21, 36, 79, 166, 168, 173
Miomo, 37
Molière, 138
Molino (*El Burlador de Sevilla*), 138
Montesquieu, 60, 112
Montpellier, 95
Moor's head, crest of Corsica, 116
Moulin Mattei, 42
Morosaglia, 57
    museum, 60
    Paoli's birthplace, 60
    tomb, 60
motorists' itinerary, 15, 17, 56, 65, 69, 74, 161, 172–84
mountaineering, 164
Mozart, 31, 138
murex shellfish, 50
Murillo, 28
Mycenae, 67

Naples, 43, 109, 110, 112
Napoleon family (*see* Bonaparte)
Napoleon III, 97
Nebbio, 50, 142–3
Nebbio, Giovanninello di, 137
Nelson, Horatio, 126
Nonza, 34, 46
    black rock, 46
    miraculous fountain, 47
    Ste-Julie, 46
North Africa, 12, 20, 29, 47, 53, 62–3, 70, 75, 84

Odysseus, 67
Office of St George, 106, 139
Ornano, Vannina d', 107
Orezza, 61–2
    Franciscan friary, 61–2
    meeting place of Napoleon and Paoli, 61
    mineral spring, 61
Orezza, Congress of, 113
Ospédale, Forêt de l', 150, 182
Ostrogoths, 10, 52–3, 137
Ota, Capo d', 126

Paccard, 97

Index

package tours, 156–8
Palaggiu, 90, 180
Palmarella, Col de, 183
Paoli, Clemente (elder brother), 110
Paoli, Giacinto (father), 60, 107–9
Paoli, Pasquale, 11, 16, 42, 43, 45, 93, 95, 104, 107, 109, 137, 140, 184
  appearance, 112
  'assasination of the bust' scandal, 116
  birth, 60
  character, 112–13
  death in London, 116
  education in Naples, 60–1, 112
  Elba, 110
  exile, 60, 111, 112, 113, 116
  family home, 60
  leader of Corsica, 110–16
  library, 60
  London, 111
  political philosophy, 112–13
  relations with Britain, 114–16
Paomia, 133, 134
Parc Naturel Régional (PNR), 13, 66, 153, 164
Paris, 95, 101, 155
Patrimonio, 47, 184
Perpignon, 107
Persians, 49
petrol, 162
Phocaea, Asia Minor, 49
Phoenicians, 137
Piana, 134, 177, 183
pieds-noirs, 64
  (*see also* North Africa)
pievi, 54
Pigno, Serra di, 34
Pinarello, 181
Pino, 45
Pirelli, 181
Pisa, 11, 22, 50, 62, 70, 105, 137
Pisan churches, 54–7, 88, 104, 142–3
Pliny, 50
Plutarch, 60
Ponape, 130
Ponte Leccia, 57, 58, 60, 121–2, 176
Ponte-Nuovo, 113
Pope, Alexander, 60
Porta, Giacomo della, 100

Porto, 12, 121, 123–33, 148, 157, 158, 177, 183
  Capo Cenino, 125, 127
  eucalyptus forest, 125, 131
  Genoese fort, 127
  Girolta, 130–1, 177
  Golfe de Girolta, 129
  Golfe de Porto, 125, 129, 133, 135, 154, 177
  La Scandola, 128–30, 135, 154
  les Calanche, 125, 133, 134–5, 154
  Monte Cenino, 129
  Ota, 126
  Porto river, 126, 127
Porto-Pollo, 79–80
Porto-Vecchio, 150, 153, 157, 181
Propriano, 12, 79, 157, 179
Prunelli, Gorges du, 183
Prunete, 175
public transport, 163–4
  local buses, 163
  railway, 163–4

Quenza, 182

Railway Magazine, 164
Regional Assembly, 65
Renaggiu, Alignement de, 90
restaurants, 169–70
Restonica, Gorges de la, 121, 122–3, 149, 175, 176
  Bergeries de Grottelle, 122
  Capo au Chiostro, 122
  Rotondo, 122
Rivarola, Count Domenico, 109
Rizzanèse river, 83, 86, 179, 180
Roberts, Eric, 164
Rocca, Rinuccio della, 106
Rocca, Sinucello della, 105–6
Roccapina, 180
Rogliano, 41
Romans, 11, 48–53, 62, 63, 70, 77, 80, 137, 140, 142
Rome, 43, 45
Roquefort cheese, 165
Rossini, 30
Rotondo, 122
Rousseau, 42, 112

St-Florent, 24, 108, 141–4, 184
   Gulf of St-Florent, 47
   Nebbio, 142
   old town, 142
   Pisan cathedral, 142–3
   port, 142
St Helena, 67
St Helena, island of, 35, 95, 101
St Ives, 44
St Pancras cemetery, London, 60
St Theophil, 117–18
San Lorenzo, 176
San-Martino-di-Loto, 36–7
San Parteo, 56–7
San Petrone, Monte, 59
Ste-Lucie, Col de, 45
Ste-Lucie-de-Porto-Vecchio, 181
Ste-Lucie-de-Tallano, 181
Santa Maria-Figaniella, 88, 180
Sagone, Golfe de, 177
Sanguinaires, Iles, 93, 102–3
Saracens, 47, 53, 54, 70, 104
Sardinia car-ferry, 161
Sartène, 13, 15, 53, 79, 83–6, 179
   Hôtel de Ville, 86
   Le Catenacciu procession, 84–5
   old town (Santa Anna), 86
   Place de la Libération, 85–6
   Ste-Marie, 84
Sausalito, 44
Scala di Sta-Regina, 121, 125–6, 149, 177
Scandola, La, 128–30, 154, 177
schist, 37, 58, 149
Scopamène, Serra-di-, 182
Semana Santa, Seville, 85
Seneca, 45–6
séparatistes
   (see *Front de libération nationale de la Corse*)
Sermano, 122, 176
Serra, Col de, 42
Seville, 138, 85
Shardanes, 82
shepherd, Corsican, 151
Shikoku island, Japan, 14
shopping, 170

Sisco, 38–40
   Ste-Catherine, 39–40
   St-Marton, 40
Société Nationale Maritime Corse-Méditerranée (SNCM), 159–60
   fares, 160
   Guide du Passager, 159
   London office, 159
   motor bikes and bicycles, 160
Solenzara, 181
SOMIVAC, 63
Sorba, Forêt de, 150, 182
Southward Ho!, 92
spelling of Corsican names, 16
Spelunca, Gorges de, 125, 126, 177
Spin' A Cavallu bridge, 86–7, 179
Spinola, Bishop Rafael, 76
Stello, Monte, 34, 38
summer holiday information, 156–8
Swift, Jonathan, 60

tasting wines, 167–8
Tavera, 182
Tavignano, Gorges de, 149
Tavignano river, 175
Teghime, Col de, 47, 184
Templars, 76
terrorism
   (see *Front de libération nationale de la Corse*)
Thrale, Mrs, 111
Tiepolo, 31
Titian, 96
Tizzano, 180
Torreens, 11, 82–3, 90, 91
Toulon, 29, 95
tourism, 12, 63, 66, 68, 136, 141
Tunisia, 109
Tyrrhenian purple dye, 50

Urban V, Pope, 54

Vaccia, Col de la, 182
Valdo-Niello, Forêt de, 126, 177
Valéry, Paul, 37
Valinco, Gulf of, 79, 107, 157, 178
Vandals, 11, 52–3, 137

Velia, 50
Venezuela, 40
Verde, Col de, 182
Vergio, Col de, 126, 148, 177
Veronese, 96
Vico, 133
Vietnamese, 86
visas for France, 155–6
Vivario, 182
Vizzavona, 182
von Neuhof, Theodor, 109

walking, 153, 164
wall-paintings in churches, 59
war memorials, 138–9

when to visit Corsica, best seasons, 158–9
wine, Corsican, 21–2, 166–8
  Ajaccio, 167
  Balagne, 167
  Cap Corse, 36, 167
  'house wines', 157, 167–8
  Patrimonio, 47, 166
  Sartène, 167
winter motoring, 163
World War, Second, 29–30, 47, 48, 61

Zicavo, 182
Zonza, 181, 182